THE BLASTED PINE

Revised and enlarged edition

THE BLASTED PINE

REVISED AND ENLARGED EDITION

An Anthology of Satire
Invective and Disrespectful Verse
Chiefly by Canadian Writers
Selected, Arranged and Introduced by

F. R. SCOTT and A. J. M. SMITH

TORONTO
THE MACMILLAN COMPANY OF CANADA LIMITED

Original edition first printed in 1957
Second printing 1960
Third printing 1962
Fourth printing 1965
This revised edition first printed in 1967

Reprinted 1971,1976

Printed in Canada for
The Macmillan Company of Canada
70 Bond Street, Toronto
M5B 1X3

ISBN 0-7705-0280-6

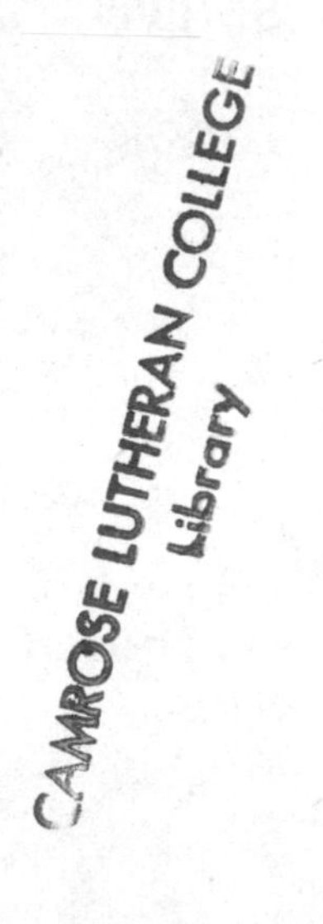

THE PROGRESS OF SATIRE

(To F.R.S. and A.J.M.S.)

Reading a dead poet
Who complained in his time
Against bad laws, bad manners,
And bad weather in bad rhyme,

I thought how glad he'd be
To be living in our time
To damn worse laws, worse manners,
And worse weather in worse rhyme.

LOUIS DUDEK

CONTENTS

I. PROLOGUE

II. TRUE PATRIOT LOVE

III. SOLID CITIZENS

IV. SNOW, DUST, HAIL AND RUST

V. THE PURSE-PROUD PRELATE

VI. INDIGENOUS THROSTLES

VII. WE STAND ON GUARD

VIII. PRIVATE HELLS

INTRODUCTION

I

"Satire, invective, and disrespectful verse" describes accurately enough what may seem to some readers a rather curious mixture of poetry, doggerel, light verse, comic rhymes, and well aimed spitballs. Traditionally, satire and invective are a method of exposing folly to the ridicule of reasonable men and vice to the condemnation of virtuous and responsible men. John Dryden put it well when he wrote, "The true end of satire is the amendment of vice by correction" (i.e., by administration of the cane), but he added a necessary reminder when he continued, "He who writes honestly is no more an enemy to the offender, than the physician to the patient, when he prescribes harsh remedies to an inveterate disease."

This is the justification of most of the pieces collected here. All of them, or nearly all of them—there are a few amusing, ridiculous, or delightful "sports" that fall outside our categories—are sharply critical, in one way or another, of some aspect of Canadian life that has more often been accepted uncritically. They have been chosen because they sound a sour note. Their tone is harsh, sometimes unrefined, sometimes, perhaps, distorted, but always unsentimental—the noise that common sense makes, or the whisper of intelligence. It is a note which has generally been drowned out in the diapason of praise with which Canadian poets have hymned the glories of the True North Strong and Free.

The voice of the dissenter, however, has never been quite silent. It has always performed the useful function of an opposition party—though of necessity not a loyal one. The first function of the kind of criticism that is immediately useful in the early stages of any reform, whether in the field of morals, manners, social customs, or politics, is to be *destructive*. Constructive criticism is all very well at a later stage, or if the thing criticized is merely superficial—error, not sin. But the most effective attack is the sharpest attack. Intensity, bitterness, and passion, then, are the qualities by which the excellence of satire and invective is to be measured. A kind of rough strength and a personal tang—the body odour of indignation—give a validity and virtue even to crude rhymes and popular doggerel.

The force of this collection is strengthened by the wide net we have drawn. Amateur writers, men of affairs, journalists, politicians, and plain people—farmers, settlers, business men, and (more recently) professors—are here, along with the established poets. And while there are a number of beautiful and deeply-felt pieces that are excellent as poetry (Lampman's *City of the End of Things*, Marriott's *Prairie Graveyard*, Mandel's *Estevan, Saskatchewan*, to name the first that come to mind) there are many that derive their strength from being nothing more than they frankly proclaim themselves to be—comic, grotesque, or simply casual. There are a few things here too that nobody would maintain are anything but bad poetry. But there is bad poetry, and bad poetry; and there is such a thing as "good" bad poetry. The verses by O'Grady, McLachlan, and Glendinning in the early days are sometimes of this sort. So are those by their close relative, Sarah Binks. They are as well worth reading as the more vaporous rhapsodies of the Maple Leaf school of patriotic nature poets.

The student of Canadian history will discover a curious truth if he places these verses in their historical setting. He will discover that it is the critics, objectors, and nay-sayers, not the conformists, who are most often in advance of their time, who most accurately foreshadow new developments and point the direction in which the reluctant conservative is going to be dragged. The reason is that the malcontent is almost invariably a realist, with his eye fixed steadily on a concrete grievance, while the cheerful enthusiast is generally a sentimental idealist. There are exceptions, of course. But one of the most genuine sources of interest in a collection like this is the opportunity it gives us of watching the operations of the critical spirit throughout nearly a century and a half of our national development. There is in these pages a brief history of Canadian thought; the poems expose an idea or a form of behaviour to public ridicule, and at the same time assert the superiority of the alternative view implied by the attack. For this reason the time of original publication of each poem is important; opinions which today seem dated or even quaint are of interest when they first appear in their historical context.

II

The critical spirit, when it finds expression in satire and invective, may be distinguished by its point of view, purpose, and direction of aim, into one of two classes: the classical or conservative, and the romantic or revolutionary. The satirist in a classical age directs his wit or anger against the nonconformist, the sectarian, and the eccentric—against all, that is, who diverge from the norm of rational behaviour and social agreeableness. In an age of well established order everybody knows what this is. The satirist then is orthodox and respectable, an exponent of fixed and generally respected principles of right feeling, correct thinking, and proper behaviour. Such satire is not likely to develop very strongly in a colony, except in the hands of a few Tory administrators, wealthy land-holders, and Church-of-England clergymen in the earliest period.

In a time of social change, such as occurred with the industrial revolution and the romantic revival (strange but inevitable concatenation!) or after World War I and the Great Depression, satire launches its attack from a different point of view, at a different target, and with a different purpose. It is now the turn of the individualist, the revolutionary, and the eccentric; and he pits himself against the established system of convention and privilege. No longer the voice of society and reason, he is one crying in the wilderness, and his critical intelligence and righteous indignation shine like bright lamps in a bleak world. It is satire of this sort that we shall find mainly, though not quite exclusively, in this book. It is the voice of a few isolated, sharp-sighted, sharp-tongued plain-speakers that we hear most often chastising, complaining, declaiming, or singing in the following pages. It is a little surprising that there have not been more of them.

We are a new country asserting its individuality against the traditions of the past. Is not the act of emigration itself a kind of satire—a romantic, indeed a revolutionary rejection of an established order? The emigrant discards an old life in favour of another to be established in a new land. Yet the English and Scottish emigrants from the Old Country—to say nothing of the United Empire Loyalists—were usually just that—emigrants, not immigrants, and the efforts they made in their new home to imitate and re-establish the attitudes and habits of the old have given to later generations of Canadians their most truly national subject of satire and irony. This accounts for the presence here of so much criticism of bourgeois respectability, Tory imperialism, mercantile or sectarian hypocrisy, and complacent materialism.

What almost all our satirists stand against is conformity of one kind or another. The verses included here, whether satirical or not, are pessimistic and destructive, and whether on a personal, social, or metaphysical level, they are all subversive—distinguished by an absence of that helpful, optimistic cheerfulness that is generally thought to be a duty nowadays. The poets and versifiers we have brought together are men who have looked behind the façade of conventional acceptance and—in most of these poems at least—have refused to play the game. In doing so, they have taken what we are compelled to describe, in old-fashioned terms, as a moral stand.

All satire, indeed, and most invective, is moral: it asserts or implies a standard of value. It makes judgments, and demands or seizes the right of self-assertion. It takes sides, speaks out, and enters actively into social, political, or moral engagements. It is a form of action, and its writers are partisans. They are very much needed in Canada today—and tomorrow.

As we wrote these lines our eyes fell on a paragraph in the *Canadian Forum* for March 1957. We write it into the record as a pertinent text on which to close. Here it is:

Walter L. Gordon, chairman of the Royal Commission on Canada's Economic Prospects, told the Canadian Club of Toronto that Canadians 25 years from now may live in an era of conformity, doing and seeing the same things, driving the same kind of cars, living in the same kind of houses and thinking the same kind of thoughts. He could not see the times producing a reassuring crop of critics and debunkers and people who are independent and individualistic in their thinking and in their approach to life. "It is hard to see," he concluded, "where they are to come from in this comfortable, complacent and conforming age."

Is it too sanguine to hope that the verses collected in *The Blasted Pine* may be admitted as evidence that the non-conformist, individual spirit has never been without its manifestations in Canada, and that in the future the stubborn, subversive, intelligent reaction to the standardized life will continue to find a voice—at least from our poets and artists?

Will anyone listen?

NOTE TO REVISED EDITION

In the ten years that have elapsed since the publication of the first edition of this anthology the writing of satirical, irreverent, and disrespectful verse has by no means abated in Canada. Our poets, young and old, continue to find enough of the pompous and ridiculous in the Canadian scene to prompt their laughter or excite their indignation. Mr. Gordon's fears that the crop of "critics and debunkers" would come to extinction seem so far to be unfounded. Indeed in recent years Canadian poetry has flourished as never before, and among the hardiest of its flowers have been those that fall within the scope of satire. The time has come therefore to bring our blastings up to date by the inclusion of work by such poets as Leonard Cohen, Henry Beissel, Margaret Atwood, Al Purdy, Alden Nowlan, Peter Miller, and George Bowering, and to fire another salvo in the long war of wit against complacency, a warfare that has not become any the less urgent in this year of centennial celebration.

The reader will notice, however, that the objects our newer poets satirize are not very different from those lambasted in the first edition. Our added authors only occasionally uncover new territory but they do bring a fresh vision to a familiar landscape. Perhaps this is only another way of saying that the Canada seen through these "improved binoculars" has not greatly changed in the last ten years. True, we have poems on Stratford, on McLuhanism, on Castro's Cuba, and on tourism, but the greatest event that seems to cry out for satire—the French-English confrontation in Quebec—is too recent and too inchoate to have found its way into poetry, or at least into poetry written in English. Only Howard Fast's "The Nature of Canadian Geology" touches briefly and ever so lightly on this theme.

It is perhaps inevitable that the objects satirized by one generation should seem less meaningful to the next. As the memory of events, powerfully impressed upon contemporaries, fades into the past, the satirical verses produced by these events lose some of their intensity. A lively appreciation of the poems in this anthology requires (and sometimes helps to impart) a knowledge of Canadian history and social customs. *The Blasted Pine* might well be recommended as required reading in university courses in Canadian government, politics, sociology, and history. We know from the reception the first edition was accorded that there is a modest audience—but a sophisticated one—that will indeed listen to what our satirists are saying.

I. PROLOGUE

CANADA: CASE HISTORY

This is the case of a high-school land,
deadset in adolescence,
loud treble laughs and sudden fists,
bright cheeks, the gangling presence.
This boy is wonderful at sports
and physically quite healthy;
he's taken to church on Sunday still
and keeps his prurience stealthy.
He doesn't like books except about bears,
collects new coins and model planes
and never refuses a dare.
His Uncle spoils him with candy, of course,
yet shouts him down when he talks at table.
You will note he's got some of his French mother's looks,
though he's not so witty and no more stable.
He's really much more like his father and yet
if you say so he'll pull a great face.
He wants to be different from everyone else
and daydreams of winning the global race.
Parents unmarried and living abroad,
relatives keen to bag the estate,
schizophrenia not excluded,
will he learn to grow up before it's too late?

EARLE BIRNEY

FROM COLONY TO NATION

A dull people,
but the rivers of this country
are wide and beautiful

A dull people
enamoured of childish games,
but food is easily come by
and plentiful

Some with a priest's voice
in their cage of ribs: but
on high mountain-tops and in thunderstorms
the chirping is not heard

Deferring to beadle and censor;
not ashamed for this,
but given over to horseplay,
the making of money

A dull people, without charm or ideas,
settling into the clean empty look
of a Mountie or dairy farmer
as into a legacy

One can ignore them
(the silences, the vast distances help)
and suppose them at the bottom
of one of the meaner lakes,
their bones not even picked for souvenirs.

IRVING LAYTON

COLD COLLOQUY

(From POEM ON CANADA)

What are you . . .? they ask, in wonder.
And she replies in the worst silence of all her woods:
I am Candida with the cane wind.

What are you . . .? they ask again, their mouths full of gum,
their eyes full of the worst silence of the worst winter in a
hundred years
and the frames of their faces chipped round the skaters' picture—
What are you . . .? they ask.
And she replies: I am the wind that wants a flag.
I am the mirror of your picture

until you make me the marvel of your life.
Yes, I am one and none, pin and pine, snow and slow,
America's attic, an empty room,
a something possible, a chance, a dance
that is not danced. A cold kingdom.

Are you a dominion of them? they ask, scurrying
home on street-cars, skiing the hill's shoulder
and hurrying where the snow is heaping colder and colder.
Are you a dominion of them? they ask.
Most loyal and empirical, she says, in ice ironic,
and subject of the king's most gratuitous modesty, she says.
What do you do then?
Lumbering is what I do and whitening is what I wheat,
but I am full of hills and sadness;
snow is where I drift and wave my winds
and as silence my doom, distance is my dream.
Mine are the violet tones of the logs in rivers,
my tallness is the tallness of the pines and the grain elevators
tubular by the scarps of coal, at Quebec.
My caves are the caves of ice but also the holes of Cartier
where the poor squat, numb with winter,
and my poverty is their rags and the prairies' drought.

What is the matter then . . .? they ask, and some are indifferent,
What is the matter then . . .? they ask.
The matter is the sections and the railways, she replies,
and the shouting lost by the way and the train's whistle
like wild-life in the night.
The matter is the promise that was never taken, she replies,
above your heads the cool and giant air
and the future aching round you like an aura—
land of the last town and the distant point,
land of the lumber track losing itself
petering out in the birches, the half-wish
turning back in the wastes of winter or slums
and the skiers lovely and lonely upon the hills
rising in domes of silence. The matter is

the skiers, she replies, athletically lonely,
drowsed in their delight, who hunt and haunt
the centres of their silence and excitement:
finding the cirrus on the high sierras
sluice down the dangers of their dear content—
the matter is being lost in a dream of motion
as larks are in their lights, or bees and flies
glued on the hump-backed honey of summer-time.

What should we do then, what should we do . . .? they ask,
out of the factories rattling a new war,
on all the Sundays time has rocked to motion.
What should we do then . . .? they ask, English and French,
Ukrainians, Poles, Finns, at drugstore corners
of streets extended to the ultimate seas
of their defended but ambiguous city.
—Suffer no more the vowels of Canada
to speak of miraculous things with a cleft palate—
let the Canadian,
with glaciers in his hair, straddle the continent,
in full possession of his earth and north
dip down his foot and touch the New York lights
or stir the vegetable matter of the Bahamas
within the Carib gutter. Let
the skiers go with slogans of their eyes
to crowd a country whose near neighbourhood's
the iron kindness of the Russian coasts—
through deserts of snow or dreary wastes of city,
the empty or the emptily crowded North.

And see, she says, the salmon pointing home
from the vast sea, the petalled plethora
and unplumbed darkness of the sea, she says:
gliding along their silvery intuitions
like current on its cables, volt upon volt,
to flash at last, sparking the mountain falls
of Restigouche—spawning a silver million.

PATRICK ANDERSON

FOUND OBJECT

"The retreat of the ice
left Canada much
in its present condition,
except for certain
post-glacial changes of level
which seem to be
still in progress."

"Canada"
Encyclopaedia Britannica
(Eleventh Edition)
1910
Volume Five
Page 143

JOHN ROBERT COLOMBO

NATIONAL IDENTITY

The Canadian Centenary Council
Meeting in Le Reine Elizabeth
To seek those symbols
Which will explain ourselves to ourselves
Evoke unlimited responses
And prove that something called Canada
Really exists in the hearts of all
Handed out to every delegate
At the start of proceedings
A portfolio of documents
On the cover of which appeared
In gold letters
            not
A Mari Usque Ad Mare
            not
Dieu Et Mon Droit
            not
Je Me Souviens
            not
E Pluribus Unum
            but
COURTESY OF COCA-COLA LIMITED.

F. R. SCOTT

II. TRUE PATRIOT LOVE

SONG

(From THE EMIGRANT)

Old England is eaten by knaves,
  Yet her heart is all right at the core,
May she ne'er be the mother of slaves,
  Nor a foreign foe land on her shore.

I love my own country and race,
  Nor lightly I fled from them both,
Yet who would remain in a place
  Where there's too many spoons for the broth.

The squire's preserving his game,
  He says that God gave it to him,
And he'll banish the poor without shame,
  For touching a feather or limb.

The Justice he feels very big,
  And boasts what the law can secure,
But has two different laws in his wig,
  Which he keeps for the rich and the poor.

The Bishop he preaches and prays,
  And talks of a heavenly birth,
But somehow, for all that he says,
  He grabs a good share of the earth.

Old England is eaten by knaves,
  Yet her heart is all right at the core,
May she ne'er be the mother of slaves,
  Nor a foreign foe land on her shore.

ALEXANDER McLACHLAN

YOUNG CANADA

Ye hopeful youth of Canada,
  Attend unto my ditty,
Ye'll find there's truth in 't, tho' it may
  Be neither wise nor witty,
But first let's throw the beaver up,
  And talk as tall 's the steeple,
That all the lower world may know,
  We are a mighty people.

We claim the new inventions in
  The art of public robbing,
And for an infant colony,
  We beat the world at jobbing;
We've quacks of every calibre,
  From him who sells the gum drug,
To him who in the rostrum stands,
  And preaches up his humbug . . .

The good old souls believe in God,
  And in a church we joke at,
But our belief is in the bank,
  And in the breeches pocket;
Old superstition vainly tries
  To frighten and enslave us,
For our new Gospel plainly says
  'Tis science that can save us . . .

'Tis money rules the world now,
  It's rank and education,
It's power and knowledge, sense and worth,
  And pious reputation.
Get cash, and 'gainst all human ills,
  You're armed and you're defended,
For in it even here on earth,
  All heaven is comprehended . . .

Buy up town lots, start shaving shops,
And issue out your paper,
A bank's a bank, altho' it be
A bank of wind and vapor;
The world is filled with pigeons, and
Your business is to pluck them,
And what were the goats sent for here,
But that the wise might suck them?

Now all the rowdies in the land,
Around you, you must gather,
By soft sawder and whiskey punch!
You are a City Father,
And having grown by villainy,
To such exalted stature,
Set up your beaver, now you're fit
To be a Legislator.

And with the wind in all your sails,
Your star in the ascendant,
The next thing you must do, is cram
The *Free and Independent*;
Play your election cards aright,
By bribery and lying,
And into Parliament you go,
With all your colours flying.

And now you take your rightful place,
Among the sons of Mammon,
The full-grown representatives
Of humbug and of gammon;
Your genius now can show itself,
You're in your proper station,
By plucking pigeons you have learned
The way to pluck the nation.

Get some fat office, for you know
Man cannot live by suction,

And then retire to your nest,
  And fatten on corruption;
Then you may sit and take your ease,
  Nor be by care affected,
A good old grey-haired patriarch,
  By all the world respected.

At last when in the grave you're laid,
  The green turf growing o'er you,
Your epitaph will be a lie,
  As big as e'er you swore to:
"A Legislator slumbers here,
  Whose heart was all affection,
He served mankind, and died in hope
  Of a joyful resurrection."

ALEXANDER McLACHLAN

PLACES

As Bees, on Flowers alighting, cease their Hum,
So, settling upon Places, Whigs grow dumb.

JOSEPH HOWE (?)

THE MEMBER OF PARLIAMENT

In years he hadn't read a book
  And boasted this at every chance,
But he possessed a knowing look
  And silver jingled in his pants.

And when bright silver jingles there
  Election is a simple thing;
But you must love the Lord and swear
  You will be true to England's king.

And honourable Josiah Boyd
  Could wave a flag and all of that

And this made up for any void
Beneath the honoured member's hat.

Sometimes he squirmed when cultured men
Revealed his grossness with intent;
But he felt quite at home again
When he sat down in parliament.

He banged his desk as any lad,
And loved to make the page-boys run;
And hoped the galleries would be glad
To look at him—their favourite son.

He stole, and boasted of his swag.
And, when his victims would rebel,
He wrapped himself in England's flag
And sang, "God Save the King", like Hell.

WILSON MacDONALD

BATTLE OF YONGE STREET, 1837

(Parody on HOHENLINDEN)

1

On Yonge street, ere the sun arose,
Stood the Queen's forces and her foes,
With many a pale and bloodless nose,
And cheeks as chill as charity.

2

But Yonge street saw another sight,
When loyal Scarboro's men of fight,
With Torrance swearing all his might,
March'd up against the enemy.

3

Tantarara! the trumpet bray'd,
Thump went gun and carronade;

The rebel rout, asham'd, dismay'd,
To right about wheel'd cleverly.

4

Smash, dash, crash! tumble, cuff and kick!
A head was broke at every lick;
With rifle squirt and bayonet prick,
The work was sharp and summary.

5

Deep rankling hate and vengeful ire
O'er Yonge street spread destruction dire,
And ruin mounts in flaming fire
The turrets of Montgomery.

6

What pen of poet shall portray
The scene on that disastrous day?
Rider and horse together lay
Weltering in war's dread revelry.

7

'Tis past: the wintry tempests sweep
O'er the cold couch where warriors sleep,
And mothers mourn and widows weep
The flower of Markham's chivalry.

ALEX. GLENDINNING

A WORD TO THE FINNIGANS

1

Let the Finnigans come,
Like the legions of Rome;
Let them tread on our borders by night or by day,
We've a bullet of lead
For each vagabond's head,
And a hole in a swamp to stow him away!

2

Scum of humanity,
Have they the vanity,
Bog-trotting, Bull-Running renegades, psha!
To think they can any day
Conquer young Canada,
Pillage our homesteads, and dictate our law?

3

Is their wrath at the full
For a brush with John Bull?
Cross the fishpond, why not, and at once go to work,
Blow his batt'ries sky high,
Knock his gunboats to pi,
And float Ireland across to the bay of New York.

4

Surely we never wrong'd them
Nor one that belong'd them;
I see no good reason for pouncing on us—
Their pleasure be done,
But as sure as a gun,
If they cross the St. Clair they'll get into a muss.

5

Draw a tight bead on them,
Crack at the head o' them;
Down wi' the ruffians, and pound them like snakes:
Base tatterdemalions,
Rips, roughs and rapscallions,
What business have they on this side of the lakes?

ALEX. GLENDINNING

DAMN YANKEES, 1830

All hail! Columbia's forests green;
All hail! New York, of cities queen;
All hail! to Jonathan, our frien';

But, lovel me!
What curious coons! how lank, how lean
Them Yankees be!

Bare-faced, din, thin, cadaverous sights!
They look as if they'd lien for nights
Deep underneath Carlanrick heights,
Or Borthwick wa's,
Then bolted up for mortal frights
To scare the craws.

These are the freemen—these the fellows
Who boast that they can buy and sell us!
They whip John Bull! and John, they tell us,
Whips every nation;
But they're as windy as the bellows,
They lee like station.

They whip the British! they, the knaves!
The maist they whip's three million slaves—
Twa thirds black niggers, and the laves
Their ain py'd rout,
Bred up and driven to fairs, Gude save's!
Like sheep and nowt.

ALEX. GLENDINNING

LE TOMBEAU DE PIERRE FALCON

Pierre Falcon,
You say here along with this unsingable music
That on June nineteenth these Burnt Wood people
Ah yes, the Métis were dark, so called Bois-Brûlés,
Arrived near this settlement of Lord Selkirk's
Fort Douglas.

You say in this second verse that your Burnt Woods
Took three foreigners prisoner at Frog Plain.
These foreigners were Scotchmen from the Orkneys

Who had come, as you put it, to rob your—Pierre
Falcon's—
Country.

Well we were just about to unhorse
When we heard two of us give, give voice.
Two of our men cried, "Hey! Look back, look back!
The Anglo-Sack
Coming for to attack."

Right away smartly we veered about
Galloping at them with a shout!
You know we did trap all, all those Grenadiers!
They could not move
Those horseless cavaliers.

Now we like honourable men did act,
Sent an ambassador—yes, in fact!
"Monsieur Governor! Would you like to stay?
A moment spare—
There's something we'd like to say."

Governor, Governor, full of ire.
"Soldiers!" he cries, "Fire! Fire!"
So they fire the first and their muskets roar!
They almost kill
Our ambassador!

Governor thought himself a king.
He wished an iron rod to swing.
Like a lofty lord he tries to act.
Bad luck, old chap!
A bit too hard you whacked!

When we went galloping, galloping by
Governor thought that he would try
For to chase and frighten us Bois-Brûlés.
Catastrophe!
Dead on the ground he lay.

Dead on the ground lots of grenadiers too.
Plenty of grenadiers, a whole slew.
We've almost stamped out his whole army
    Of so many
    Five or four left there be.

You should have seen those Englishmen—
Bois-Brûlés chasing them, chasing them.
From bluff to bluff they stumbled that day
    While the Bois-Brûlés
    Shouted "Hurray!"

And now in this eleventh verse you ask
Who made up this song and then you tell us
That you yourself made it up—Pierre Falcon.
You made it up to sing the glory of the
Burnt Wood People.

Far away and dear, spunky old and early poet
I wish I could sing the praises of the Neon People
To You.

JAMES REANEY

TO TENNYSON

I

On his Acceptance of a Peerage

Just for a handful of silver he left us,
Just for a ribbon to stick in his coat.
BROWNING

You take the title as a dog a bone,
  Who should have met the offer with a sneer,
  'Tis with regret we hail thee as a peer,
And see thy servile clinging to the throne.
On royalty fawn parasites alone—
  Squeak not of freedom, Alfred Vere de Vere!
  Thy senile voice grows weaker year by year,
Soon o'er thee will oblivion's dust be thrown.

Forgotten is the once-famed laureate crew—
  Rowe, Eusden, Shadwell, Warton, Cibber, Tate,
  And others who like slaves on kings did wait.
Who reads voluminous Southey? Mighty few!
A pigmy thou when memory brings to view
  Immortal glories of the vanished great,
  Whose fame the centuries keep inviolate;
Such will not be, my lord, the fate of you.

Pipe on for pay, court-toady of St. James!
For present praise, thy meed ephemeral fame's,
Dan Chaucer, Milton, Shelley,—each high name
Puts thine effeminate mild muse to shame.
Sing with grace courtly, and Virgilian mien
Of still life, parlour pathos, garden scene;
Of languid lilies, zephyrs, minster towers,
Praise brainless princes, maudlin dukes, for these
Are themes whereto thy grovelling spirit warms,
And the more congenial to thy paltry powers.
Thou canst not sing the splendour of the seas,
The mountain's grandeur or the sweeping storm's!

II

On his Last Poem (?) on Freedom

Doddered with age.

DRYDEN

Seeming devotion does but gild a knave.

WALLER

Still, still you whang your gentle muse,
  O noble (?) coroneted bard!
Your verse is—('twould disgrace the stews)
  Worth about fifty cents a yard.

Prate not of freedom, poor old man!
  Now that your star is on the wane;
True Freedom—life Republican—
  Has worthier lyres to sing her strain.

You damned her with faint praise when young,
  You loved her not as love the brave;
Your feeble untempestuous tongue
  Will scarcely "sing her to her grave".

Pipe on of court and parlour scene,
  And eulogize the worldly-great;
Trot out your lifeless plays inane,
  And let them find oblivion's fate.

Let others praise in deathless verse
  Cromwellian England—Milton's pride;
You would but dance behind the hearse
  If Liberty forever died.

Let others praise triumvirate Rome,
  Her splendour, power, and elegance;
And fairer than imperial dome
  The beauty of free modern France.

Let others of proud Athens sing,
  When Pericles and arts and arms
Did unto her great glory bring,
  And of Aspasia's peerless charms—

The uncrowned queen whom the gods graced
  With Pallas' gifts, and Cypris' form:
No love-dream phantoms fairer-faced
  In poets' fancies e'er did swarm.

Prate not of Freedom, throne-tied bard!
  'Twill need your help—the tottering crown.
Coax up your Pegasus, my lord,
  And descant on defunct John Brown.

JUDSON FRANCE

THE PRINCE'S VISIT

A Humorous Description

Of

THE TOUR OF HIS ROYAL HIGHNESS, THE

PRINCE OF WALES,

THROUGH THE UNITED STATES OF

AMERICA, IN 1860

PART I

NEWFOUNDLAND TO NEW YORK

(Extract)

Already the tidings have flashed o'er the land.
The Nobs of Cape Breton have shaken his hand;
The Prince Edward's people have met him with awe;
The Chief of Newfoundland extended a paw;
The loyal Blue-noses a welcome have blown,
To greet ALBERT EDWARD and claim him their own,—
Since, surely, they have the best right to adore him,
As having received his grandfather before him.
And as for the Canadas! Loyalty's run
Into madness almost for VICTORIA's son.
They have shown him the wonders of water and land,
And shot him down lumber-shoots awful and grand;
They have dined him, and wined him, in manner most royal.
Addressed and harangued him to prove they were loyal.
They have bored him in parks, and they've bored him in halls;
Danced him almost to death in no end of balls.
They have bored him in colleges, bored him in schools;
Convinced him that Orange fanatics are fools.
Torn his bed-clothes to strips,—every fool keeping one,
To remember the linen the PRINCE slept upon.
They have stolen his gloves, and purloined his cravat;
Even scraped a souvenir from the nap of his hat.
In short, they have followed him, hustled and shoved him.
To convince him more fully how dearly they loved him.
Each snob with a present, done up in a parcel,

To the lively disgust of the DUKE OF NEWCASTLE.
They've "received" him at church in magnificent state,
The Bishop and Clergy—all solemn, sedate,
With a farce only played on this single occasion,—
Forming a clerico-comic procession,
To show him his pew, with the utmost urbanity,
Ere they read him the Collect denouncing all vanity.
And the pew, as a matter of course, was hung
With most solemn of frippery, solemnly strung;
Surmounted, I need scarcely say, by a crown;—
But so tenderly poised, that the DUKE, with a frown,
Sat the service out in a reverie brown,
Looking up, as expecting the thing to come down.
Tho' 't would not have hurt much had it come to the ground;
Since a crown is, you know, but one fourth of a pound.

So they rode him and boated him, church'd him and speech'd him,
Feasted him, toasted him, ball'd him, and preach'd him;
And, wishing all possible honor to do him,
Made him review them, that they might review him.
While, to make matters worse, and in full execution
Of the plan which had doomed him to dread persecution,
The New York reporters all "followed him round",
Held him always in sight, and forever in sound,
To keep Mr. BENNETT religiously posted
As to what the PRINCE said when his mother was toasted,
And to let us, benighted republicans, know
Where His Highness had gone or intended to go;
How he looked when he danced—when he sat at his ease—
When His Highness had sneezed, or was going to sneeze;
Whether he smiled, or whether he laughed;
All recorded, and morning and night telegraphed,
To the end that New York might reliably know
What his dear little Princeship had done or would do.
Till, at length, when routine had most thoroughly tired him,
It struck him that Canada no longer required him.

R. J. de CORDOVA

THE ROYAL VISIT

When the King and the Queen came to Stratford
Everyone felt at once
How heavy the Crown must be.
The Mayor shook hands with their Majesties
And everyone presentable was presented
And those who weren't have resented
It, and will
To their dying day.
Everyone had almost a religious experience
When the King and Queen came to visit us
(I wonder what *they* felt!)
And hydrants flowed water in the gutters
All day.
People put quarters on the railroad tracks
So as to get squashed by the Royal Train
And some people up the line at Shakespeare
Stayed in Shakespeare, just in case—
They did stop too,
While thousands in Stratford
Didn't even see them
Because the Engineer didn't slow down
Enough in time.
And although,
But although we didn't see them in any way
(I didn't even catch the glimpse
The teacher who was taller did
Of a gracious pink figure)
I'll remember it to my dying day.

JAMES REANEY

FRANKIE WENT DOWN TO THE CORNER

(1936)

Ontario's such a respectable place;
Drinking's no crime, but it's still a disgrace,
So hide us away behind curtain and screen

While we stealthily go through the motions obscene
        In a manner genteel, correctly genteel,
Secret and stuffy, but always genteel.

Let us drink upon land, as we smoke in a train,
In places as airy and light as a drain,
Let us scuttle for cover, like bugs under shelves,
Lest people should think we're enjoying ourselves.
        Oh no, we're genteel, we're grimly genteel
(To be seen drinking gaily is far from genteel).

Though our neighbours all say, with a sneer and a snicker,
We're not man enough to stand up to our liquor,
Three cheers for the tables! A man on his feet
Can carry much less than slumped in a seat.
        Besides, it's genteel, it's very genteel;
Beer served at a table's completely genteel.

But of course if a restaurant ask us to dine
It's immoral to order a bottle of wine
—But wait! Are there six standard beds in the house?
Then away with dull care! We're all set for a souse
        For then it's genteel (beds make it genteel),
Though drunk and dyspeptic, we must be genteel.

And we can't allow music, or people might think
Our pleasure's not limited solely to drink.
So musicians may starve, but they must not appear
In the sinister presence of bottles of beer.
        For that isn't genteel, it's far from genteel;
Only a gurgle is really genteel.

"Bar" is a nasty, a horrible word.
"Taprooms" and "taverns" and "pubs" are absurd;
Give us a name with a resonant boom,
A respectable name like "Beverage Room".
        Shabby genteel, shabby genteel,
Ontario's bound to be shabby genteel.

L. A. MacKAY

AUDACITY

("Audacity is missing in Canada." *The Times* 30/11/59)

They say we lack audacity, that we are middle class, without the adventurousness that arises from the desperation of the lower classes or the tradition of the upper classes.
They say we are more emphatically middling than any country west of Switzerland, and that boldness and experiment are far from our complacent thoughts.
But I say to you, they do not know where to look, and have not the eyes to see.
For audacity is all around us,
Boldness sits in the highest places,
We are riddled with insolence.

Do you want audacity?
Let me tell you—
Any day in Montreal you may hear the guns crack at the noon-hour, as the police give chase to the bank-robbers
Who are helping themselves to the wealth of the land like the French and the English before them, *coureur-de-bois* and fur-trader rolled into one;
You may watch the patrol-cars circle their beats to gather the weekly pay-off from unlicensed cafés
Whose owners sell booze on the side to acquire the $15,000 they need for the $25 permit;
You may learn the name of the distinguished Legislative Councillor who controls the *caisse-electorale*
Into which rattles the coin that makes possible the letting of contracts,
And who tips his hat to the priest
And is saluted respectfully in return;
You may marvel at the boldness of promoters of oil and natural gas, men too quick for production, fixers and peddlers,
Getting their hands on concessions and rights, access to underground treasures awaiting man's use in the womb of our northland,

Playing the suckers and markets, turning their thousands to millions, loading the pipe-lines with overhead that is paid by the housewife who cooks her spaghetti,
Then solemnly demanding higher rates for sales of the product (extra hot, natural gas!) before friends on the Board of Control;
You may follow the hucksters and admen compiling their budgets, planning the assault on "public opinion", setting the poll-questions,
Writing editorials for weeklies, letters to editors, telegrams to Senators, articles for journals,
Day after day on the job of confusing the issue, baiting the egg-heads, laughing at the "culture kids" of CBC, fixing the give-aways,
Posing as democracy's friends and admirers, while undermining the concept of government and welfare,
Singing the praises of free enterprise that relies on high tariffs, defence contracts and floor prices;
You may stand in awe at the audacity of journalists, twisting the news items by headline and rewrite, blanking out truth,
Ponderously laying down the conventional wisdom in unconventional English,
While a few owners gather dailies into chains run by gangs of paid hack-men,
Then add on the radio stations and TV outlets, lest some glimmer of free opinion escape them;
You may be amazed at the boldness of churchmen and ministers, meeting in synod and conclave and conference to spy out our sinfulness,
Who wax indignant over lotteries, horse-racing and the drink question, or, with Savonarola intensity,
Denounce crime-comics and short bathing-suits;
But all this is as nothing, not worthy of mention,
Beside the supreme, the breath-taking audacity
Of the great executives in their panelled board-rooms
Found at every point in the social structure where policy is laid down or decision taken,
Without whom no hospital can be opened, no charitable campaign

launched, no church can engage a preacher and no university
can build a building,
Daring to be omniscient, omnipotent, omnipresent,
not to mention omnivorous—
These surely you can see in this Canada of ours, O London *Times*,
In this country that has the audacity to proclaim the "supremacy
of God"
In its Bill of Rights?

F. R. SCOTT

BALLADE OF MEDDLERS

A plague on those who would regulate
Every detail of our troubled lives!
Let's eat and drink and fight and mate
And leave to God what then survives!
Thus every man for himself contrives
His inexact best quality:
Ministers, medicals, meddlesome wives,
Go your way and let folk be!

O anxious saviours of men and such,
Thanks for your help in our evil plight!
But please don't save us all too much!
When God woke up and called for light
He set things turning from left to right,
A good enough sign it seems to me
That we shall turn thus without you—quite:
Go your way and let folk be!

For man and beast and imp and elf
One rule is writ in language terse:
Each must answer to himself
In the sequence of the universe:
And we may crawl from the primal curse
Fast if we choose, or leisurely,
But meddlers aye make matters worse:
Go your way and let folk be!

Maybe a helping hand is the best
Signal from God that ever we see:
But that's one thing, and for the rest,
Go your way and let folk be!

TOM MacINNES

THE MONARCH OF THE ID

(With apologies to Gilbert but none to the Examiner of Publications in the Customs Branch, Ottawa)

I

I am the scourge of scribbling crooks,
The Examiner of Books,
Whose might is right by the Customs Act.

Chorus
He bans every magazine of fiction or of fact,
Every drawing pornographic, every snap or pious tract,
All etchings, paintings, pamphlets, every artifact,
He bans every volume leather bound or paper backed—
That fails to pass his quiz in Moral Tact!

II

For all my salary is earned
Letting no page go unturned
To spot sedition, sex or treason.

Chorus
Whether masking as a classic or a book of rhyme or reason
Or a portrait of a lady who has not enough to please on,
He will stop them at the border and declare them out of season,
He will stamp them as fit only for Her Majesty's adhesion,
And obscene and full of blasphemy and treason!

III

Anonymous in Ottawa
I preserve the Moral Law
And impound every drop of foreign sin.

Chorus
Neither Lawrence, Farrell, Faulkner, B. McFadden or their kin,
Neither Hanley, Patchen, Joyce, *Arabian Nights* or notes therein,
Neither Panter-Downes nor Radclyffe-Hall (although as yet *East Lynne*),
Neither Balzac, Edmund Wilson, Mailer, Maupassant or Glyn,
Henry Miller, Stopes or Trotsky, Margaret Sanger or Rubin,
May import or smuggle in their verbal gin!

IV

I am the Monarch of the Id,
The keeper of the Freudian Lid,
Though my praise no man or woman chants.

Chorus
Although all things immoral he can cipher at a glance
And single handed keeps us clothed in literary pants
There's none at home nor yet abroad who honours him with chants,
Except our Cabinet Ministers, their brothers in the Manse,
Their sisters and their cousins, whom they reckon up by dozens, and their aunts!

EARLE BIRNEY

LETTER TO A LIBRARIAN

Mr. P.—I have heard it rumoured
That you, humanist, librarian with a licence,
In the shady privacy of your glassed room
Tore up my book of poems.

Sir, a word in your ear. Others
Have tried that game: burned Mann
And my immortal kinsman Heine.
Idiots! What act could be vainer?

For this act of yours, the ligatures
Pest-corroded, your eyes shall fall
From their sockets; drop on your lacquered desk
With the dull weight of pinballs.

And brighter than the sapless vine
Your hands shall flare;
To the murkiest limbos of the library
Flashing my name like a neon sign.

And the candid great
Of whom not one was ever an Australian
Cry dustily from their shelves,
"Impostor! False custodian!"

Till a stunned derelict
You fall down blind, ear-beleaguered,
While Rabelais pipes you to a wished-for death
On a kazoo quaint and silvered.

IRVING LAYTON

A LASS IN WONDERLAND

I went to bat for the Lady Chatte
Dressed in my bib and gown.
The judges three glared down at me
The priests patrolled the town.

My right hand shook as I reached for the book
And rose to play my part,
For out on the street were the marching feet
Of the League of the Sacred Heart.

The word "obscene" was supposed to mean
"Undue exploitation of sex".
This wording's fine for your needs and mine
But it's far too free for Quebec's.

I tried my best, with unusual zest,
To drive my argument through,
But I soon got stuck on what rhymes with "muck"
And that dubious word "undue".

So I raised their sights to the Bill of Rights
And cried: "Let freedom ring!",
Showed straight from the text that freedom of sex
Was as clear as anything.

Then I plunged into love, the spell that it wove,
And its attributes big and bold
Till the legal elect all stood erect
As my rapturous tale was told.

The judges' sighs and rolling of eyes
Gave hope that my case was won,
Yet Mellors and Connie still looked pretty funny
Dancing about in the sun.

What hurt me was not that they did it a lot
And even ran out in the rain,
'Twas those curious poses with harebells and roses
And that dangling daisy-chain.

Then too the sales made in the paper-back trade
Served to aggravate judicial spleen,
For it seems a high price will make any book nice
While its mass distribution's obscene.

Oh Letters and Law are found in the raw
And found on the heights sublime,
But D. H. Lawrence would view with abhorrence
This Jansenist pantomime.

F. R. SCOTT

DIALECTICS

Dialectic is our love,
study us as things that move,
watch as love to lover fits
the unity of opposites.

Low the moon and shining bright
sees our spiral joy invite
kisses to a tenser key,
quantity to quality.

While the houses sink asleep
revolutionary the leap
changes into something new
quantities of me and you.

Then at last, as still as bone,
we are lying, each alone,
"on a higher plane" and sated—
the negation is negated.

Happy on the ample bed
each in each was comforted,
yet as opposites we live
and the merging's relative.

Thus an end to lover's act
viewed as an objective fact—
Dr. Dühring must agree
practice mates with theory.

PATRICK ANDERSON

THE MODERN POLITICIAN

What manner of soul is his to whom high truth
Is but the plaything of a feverish hour,
A dangling ladder to the ghost of power!
Gone are the grandeurs of the world's iron youth,
When kings were mighty, being made by swords.
Now comes the transit age, the age of brass,
When clowns into the vacant empires pass,
Blinding the multitude with specious words.
To them faith, kinship, truth and verity,
Man's sacred rights and very holiest thing,
Are but the counters at a desperate play,
Flippant and reckless what the end may be,
So that they glitter, each his little day,
The little mimic of a vanished king.

ARCHIBALD LAMPMAN

TO A RESTLESS POLITICIAN

If you had buttocks plump and fat
you would not squirm and twist—
how odd that steatopygy
can be so sadly missed!

And when you speak in Parliament
so pointlessly, my friend,
I would your adiposity
were at your other end!

GEORGE WALTON

W. L. M. K.

How shall we speak of Canada,
Mackenzie King dead?
The Mother's boy in the lonely room
With his dog, his medium and his ruins?

He blunted us.

We had no shape
Because he never took sides,
And no sides
Because he never allowed them to take shape.

He skilfully avoided what was wrong
Without saying what was right,
And never let his on the one hand
Know what his on the other hand was doing.

The height of his ambition
Was to pile a Parliamentary Committee on a Royal
Commission.
To have "conscription if necessary
But not necessarily conscription",
To let Parliament decide—
Later.

Postpone, postpone, abstain.

Only one thread was certain:
After World War I
Business as usual,
After World War II
Orderly decontrol.
Always he led us back to where we were before.

He seemed to be in the centre
Because we had no centre,
No vision
To pierce the smoke-screen of his politics.

Truly he will be remembered
Wherever men honour ingenuity,
Ambiguity, inactivity, and political longevity.

Let us raise up a temple
To the cult of mediocrity,
Do nothing by halves
Which can be done by quarters.

F. R. SCOTT

ELECTION DAY

1

I shut the careful door of my room and leave
letters, photographs and the growing poem—
the locked zone of my tight and personal thought
slough off—recede from down the green of the street.
Naked almost among the trees and wet—
a strike for lightning.

And everything rushes at me, either fierce or friendly
in a sudden world of bulls.
Faces on posters in the leaves call out
the violent *yes* or *no* to my belief,
are quick or slow or halted to my pulse.

Oh, on this beautiful day, the weather wooing
the senses and the feel of walking
smooth in my summer legs
I lope through the tall and trembling grass and call
the streaming banner of my public colour.

2

Here in this place, the box and private privet
denote the gentleman and shut him in—
for feudally he lives and the feud on.

Colonel Evensby with his narrow feet
will cast his blue blood ballot for the Tory

and in the polling station I shall meet
the smiling, rather gentle overlords
propped by their dames and almost twins in tweeds,
and mark my X against them and observe
my ballot slip, a bounder, in the box.

And take my route again through the lazy streets
alive with all-out blossoming, through trees
that stint no colour for their early summer
and past an empty lot where an old dog
appoints himself as guardian of the green.

3

Radio owns my room as the day ends.
The slow returns begin, the voice calls
the yes's and the no's that ring or toll;
the districts all proclaim themselves in turn
and public is my room, not personal.

Midnight. I wander on the quiet street,
its green swamped by the dark; a pale glow
sifts from the distant lamps. Behind the leaves
the faces on the posters wait and blow,
tattered a little and less urgent now.

I pass the empty lot. The old dog
has trotted off to bed. The neighbourhood
is neatly hedged with privet still, the lights
are blinking out in the enormous homes.
Gentlemen, for the moment, you may sleep.

P. K. PAGE

PARLIAMENTARY LIBRARY: OTTAWA

Tier upon tier
of beautifully bound
dried-out corpses of books,
suitably entombed
in this mausoleum
they tell us is lined
with the finest hand-carved
native woods, on which
no one yet
has had the guts to carve
KILROY WAS HERE

RAYMOND SOUSTER

BUSINESS AS USUAL

The gold roof of Parliament covered
with fingerprints and scratches.
And here are the elected, hunchbacked
from climbing on each other's heads.

The most precious secret has been leaked:
There is no Opposition!

Over-zealous hacks hoist the P.M.
through the ceiling. He fools
an entire sled-load of Miss Canada losers
by acting like a gargoyle.

Some fool (how did he get in) who
wants jobs for everyone and says
so in French is quickly interred
under a choice piece of the cornice

and likes it. (STAG PARTY LAUGHTER)
When are they going to show the dirty movie?

Don't cry, Miss Canada,
it's not as though the country's
in their hands.
And next year we're piping in
Congressional proceedings
direct from Washington—
all they'll have to do
is make divorces.

LEONARD COHEN

POLITICAL MEETING

(For CAMILLIEN HOUDE)

On the school platform, draping the folding seats,
they wait the chairman's praise and glass of water.
Upon the wall the agonized Y initials their faith.

Here all are laic; the skirted brothers have gone.
Still, their equivocal absence is felt, like a breeze
that gives curtains the sounds of surplices.

The hall is yellow with light, and jocular;
suddenly someone lets loose upon the air
the ritual bird which the crowd in snares of singing

catches and plucks, throat, wings, and little limbs.
Fall the feathers of sound, like *alouette*'s.
The chairman, now, is charming, full of asides and wit,

building his orators, and chipping off
the heckling gargoyles popping in the hall.
(Outside, in the dark, the street is body-tall,

flowered with faces intent on the scarecrow thing
that shouts to thousands the echoing
of their own wishes.) The Orator has risen!

Worshipped and loved, their favourite visitor,
a country uncle with sunflower seeds in his pockets,
full of wonderful moods, tricks, imitative talk,

he is their idol: like themselves, not handsome,
not snobbish, not of the *Grande Allée! Un homme!*
Intimate, informal, he makes bear's compliments

to the ladies; is gallant; and grins;
goes for the balloon, his opposition, with pins;
jokes also on himself, speaks of himself

in the third person, slings slang, and winks with folklore;
and knows now that he has them, kith and kin.
Calmly, therefore, he begins to speak of war,

praises the virtue of being *Canadien,*
of being at peace, of faith, of family,
and suddenly his other voice: *Where are your sons?*

He is tearful, choking tears; but not he
would blame the clever English; in their place
he'd do the same; maybe.

Where *are* your sons?
The whole street wears one face,
shadowed and grim; and in the darkness rises
the body-odour of race.

A. M. KLEIN

M. BERTRAND

Oh, but in France they arrange these things much better!
M. Bertrand who always, before kissing the female wrist
rolls the *r* in *charmante*
admits he owes everything to those golden Sorbonne
years.
Returned now to our forest, he is sad and nostalgic;
indeed, pained; he winces when his brother says *icitte.*

Oh, he can never forget fair Paris, its culture and cuisine,
particularly as he stalks deaf and hungry
among the barbarians who never were seasick.
Still, he has one consolation—the visitor from abroad,
the old classmate, the *conférencier,* perhaps, even
a bearded *maître* of the Academy.
Then is he revived, like a dotard by the *Folies Bergères,*
revived, stimulated, made loquacious with *argot,*
and can't do enough for his guest, but would lavish on him
jowl-kiss, hand-kiss, and other kisses Parisian.

A. M. KLEIN

MONSIEUR GASTON

You remember the big Gaston, for whom everyone
predicted
a bad end?—
Gaston, the neighbour's gossip and his mother's cross?
You remember him *vaurien,* always out of a job,
with just enough clinking coinage
for pool, bright neckties, and blondes,—
the scented Gaston in the poolroom lolling
in meadows of green baize?
In clover now. Through politics. *Monsieur* Gaston.

They say the Minister of a certain department does
not move
without him; and they say, to make it innocent,—
chauffeur.
But everyone understands. Why, wherever our
Gaston smiles
a nightclub rises and the neons flash.
To his slightest whisper
the bottled rye, like a fawning pet-dog, gurgles.
The burlesque queen will not undress
unless Monsieur Gaston says yes.

And the Madame will shake her head behind the
curtain-rods
unless he nods.

A changed man, Gaston; almost a civil servant,
keeps records, appointments, women; speaks tough
English;
is very much respected.
You should hear with what greetings his distinguished
approach is greeted;
you should see the gifts he gets,
with compliments for his season.

A. M. KLEIN

THE WAY THE WORLD ENDS

Before me on the dancestand
A god's vomit or damned by his decrees
The excited twitching couples shook and
Wriggled like giant parentheses.

A pallid Canadienne
Raised a finger and wetted her lip,
And echoing the nickelodeon
"Chip" she breathed drowsily, "Chip, chip."

Aroused, her slavish partner
Smiled, showed his dentures through soda-pop gas,
And "chip" he said right back to her
And "chip, chip" she said and shook her ass.

Denture to denture, "Pas mal"
They whispered and were glad, jerked to and fro;
Their distorted bodies like bits of steel
Controlled by that throbbing dynamo.

They stomped, flung out their arms, groaned;
And in a flash I saw the cosmos end
And last of all the black night cover this:
"Chip, chip" and a shake of the ass.

IRVING LAYTON

BONNE ENTENTE

The advantages of living with two cultures
Strike one at every turn,
Especially when one finds a notice in an office building:
"This elevator will not run on Ascension Day";
Or reads in the *Montreal Star*:
"Tomorrow being the Feast of the Immaculate
Conception,
There will be no collection of garbage in the city";
Or sees on the restaurant menu the bilingual dish:

DEEP APPLE PIE
TARTE AUX POMMES PROFONDES

F. R. SCOTT

THE STATUS OF CANADIAN GEOLOGY

A graduate, *magna cum lava*,
Of Ottawa's College of Mines,
He died while at work in Ungava
By failing to read the French signs.

His friend from Quebec on the survey,
Refusing to eat English food,
Succumbed to pellagra and scurvy—
The ore they're interred in is crude.

NATHAN FAST

A CHURCH SEEN IN CANADA

O country doubly split! One way
Tugged eastward; one to U.S.A.:
One way tugged deep toward silver Rome;
One way scotched stubborn here at home;
What panacea for your ills?
(Le Sacré Coeur de Crabtree Mills).

THEODORE SPENCER

HOMO CANADENSIS

I didn't know him
but thought somebody else did,
for everyone was friendly in that bar
except this guy in the red checked shirt:
he was aggressive and pro-Canadian,
stubbing a Players outside the ashtray,
swaying in his chair and gulping beer
like water
drunk and getting drunker—
"Best beer in the world," he said.
"Bout the only thing left that's really Canadian."
And glared at us.
"Did you know 60% of Canadian industry
is American owned?
They callem American shubshidyaries—"
Everyone laughed when he stumbled over the word,
and he slapped his hand hard on the table,
"Don't laugh!" he said.
"Okay, I been drinkin, I like to drink.
But don't laugh when you see the country
TAKEN OVER
just sort of casually
like an afterthought, like a burp after dinner—"
"So what?" somebody said.
"Everybody here knows we'll belong to the States
in another 10 years . . ."

The guy swelled up like a sneering bullfrog,
"And guys like you deserve to be taken over.
But when you are you'll be 2nd class Americans,
like Negroes in the south, like Indians here—
You'll be 2nd class Americans because
you were never 1st class Canadians in the first place—"
Everybody stiffened.
"Okay," he said,
"I'll buy the beer and shut up."
But after a few seconds he couldn't keep quiet.
"Anybody ever hear of the San Juan Islands?
No, I guess not. Well, Canada got gypped there.
Anybody know about the Alaska Panhandle deal,
or remember the Herbert Norman case, by any chance?
Well, I'm tellin you, this country is being taken
like a glass of beer. It's a matter of economics.
And none of you guys really give a damn,
just slop your beer and wait to be taken
by some big bellied American in Washington.
And I'm tellin you, they're all greedy bastards—!"
"I like Americans," someone said mildly,
and it seemed just by chance his arm lifted,
meeting checked shirt's arm in the middle of the table.
That was all it needed:
"Okay, loud mouth, let's see you put me down!"
They call it "arm wrestling" some places:
and the yellow beer jiggled as clasped hands
pushed on elbow fulcrum—everyone watching.
The guy in the checked shirt was drunk
and the other guy more or less sober,
so it shouldn't have been much of a contest.
Their arms strained like two-thirds of a tripod,
and checked shirt put on the pressure,
"I'm tellin you they're bastards—!"
The other guy was big, but he collapsed quick,
knocking over a glass of beer and the salt shaker.
"Just shows you," checked shirt said,
looking around the table. He started to go.

"I gotta be gettin back. Be seein ya—"
"You been huntin?" somebody asked.
"That's right, up near Bancroft. Takin back a nice buck."
"Where ya from?"
Checked shirt grinned.
"New York," he said.

ALFRED PURDY

A SOVEREIGN NATION

Ours is a sovereign nation
Bows to no foreign will
But whenever they cough in Washington
They spit on Parliament Hill.

JOE WALLACE

AT THE TOURIST CENTER IN BOSTON

There is my country under glass,
a white relief—
map with red dots for the cities,
reduced to the size of a wall

and beside it 10 blownup snapshots
one for each province,
in purple-browns and odd reds,
the green of the trees dulled:
all blues however
of an assertive purity.

Mountains and lakes and more lakes
(though Quebec is a restaurant and Ontario the empty
interior of the Parliament buildings),
with nobody climbing the trails and hauling out
the fish and splashing in the water

but arrangements of grinning tourists—
look here, Saskatchewan
is a flat lake, some convenient rocks
where two children pose with a father
and the mother is cooking something
in immaculate slacks by a smokeless fire,
her teeth white as detergent.

Whose dream is this, I would like to know;
is this a manufactured
hallucination, a cynical fiction, a lure
for export only?

I seem to remember people,
at least in the cities, also slush,
machines and assorted garbage. Perhaps
that was my private mirage

which will just evaporate
when I go back. Or the citizens will be gone,
run off to the peculiarly
green forests
to wait among the brownish mountains
for the platoons of tourists
and plan their odd red massacres.

Unsuspecting
window lady, I ask you:

Do you see nothing
watching you from under the water?

Was the sky ever blue?

Who really lives there?

MARGARET ATWOOD

THE ONLY TOURIST IN HAVANA TURNS HIS THOUGHTS HOMEWARD

Come, my brothers,
let us govern Canada,
let us find our serious heads,
let us dump asbestos on the White House,
let us make the French talk English,
  not only here but everywhere,
let us torture the Senate individually
  until they confess,
let us purge the New Party,
let us encourage the dark races
  so they'll be lenient
  when they take over,
let us make the CBC talk English,
let us all lean in one direction
  and float down
  to the coast of Florida,
let us have tourism,
let us flirt with the enemy,
let us smelt pig-iron in our backyards,
let us sell snow
  to under-developed nations,
(Is it true one of our national leaders
  was a Roman Catholic?)
let us terrorize Alaska,
let us unite
  Church and State,
let us not take it lying down,
let us have two Governor Generals
  at the same time,
let us have another official language,
let us determine what it will be,
let us give a Canada Council Fellowship
  to the most original suggestion,
let us teach sex in the home
  to parents,
let us threaten to join the U.S.A.

and pull out at the last moment,
my brothers, come,
our serious heads are waiting for us somewhere
like Gladstone bags abandoned
after a coup d'état,
let us put them on very quickly,
let us maintain a stony silence
on the St. Lawrence Seaway.

Havana
April 1961

LEONARD COHEN

III. SOLID CITIZENS

THE WORKMAN'S SONG

Come all ye weary sons of toil,
  And listen to my song,
We've eat oppression's bitter bread,
  And eat it far too long.

Oh poverty's a dreadful thing,
  Her bite is always keen,
Oppression's foot is always shod,
  And greed is always mean.

The great, the greasy multitude,
  Should neither think nor feel,
They've but to lick the hand that holds
  Their noses to the wheel.

ALEXANDER McLACHLAN

ON OSTENTATION

Be assured that the splendid carriages
of your Judges and Pensioners and Governors and Gentry
will be followed by pauperism, poverty, vice and crime.
It adds to the pleasures
(mean and grovelling as they are)
of such a man as Doctor Strachan,
to have a hundred poor miserable wretches
humbly attending at his gate
or in his "soup kitchen"
begging for a morsel.
Their poverty forms *an agreeable* and striking contrast
with the coach, the palace, the liveried footman &c &c.
But I fear much it will not gild the horrors of a death bed.
History is a cheat
and experience a deceiver
if such men as Lord Eldon can sleep sweet,
and feel, in the dark and gloomy evening of life
no compunction for their crimes.

WILLIAM LYON MACKENZIE
and JOHN ROBERT COLOMBO

TO A MILLIONAIRE

The world in gloom and splendour passes by,
And thou in the midst of it with brows that gleam,
A creature of that old distorted dream
That makes the sound of life an evil cry.
Good men perform just deeds, and brave men die,
And win not honour such as gold can give,
While the vain multitudes plod on, and live,
And serve the curse that pins them down: But I
Think only of the unnumbered broken hearts,
The hunger and the mortal strife for bread,
Old age and youth alike mistaught, misfed,
By want and rags and homelessness made vile,
The griefs and hates, and all the meaner parts
That balance thy one grim misgotten pile.

ARCHIBALD LAMPMAN

FIVE-PER-CENT

Because I have ten thousand pounds I sit upon my stern,
And leave my living tranquilly for other folks to earn.
For in some procreative way that isn't very clear,
Ten thousand pounds will breed, they say, five hundred
every year.
So as I have a healthy hate of economic strife,
I mean to stand aloof from it the balance of my life.
And yet with sympathy I see the grimy son of toil,
And heartily congratulate the tiller of the soil.
I like the miner in the mine, the sailor on the sea,
Because up to five hundred pounds they sail and mine
for me.
For me their toil is taxed unto that annual extent,
According to the holy shibboleth of Five-per-Cent.

So get ten thousand pounds, my friend, in any way you can,
And leave your future welfare to the noble Working Man.
He'll buy your suits of Harris tweed, an Airedale and a car;
Your golf clubs and your morning *Times,* your whisky and
cigar.
He'll cosily install you in a cottage by a stream,
With every modern comfort, and a garden that's a dream.
Or if your tastes be urban, he'll provide you with a flat,
Secluded from the clamour of the proletariat.
With pictures, music, easy chairs, a table of good cheer,
A chap can manage nicely on five hundred pounds a year.
And though around you painful signs of industry you view,
Why should you work when you can make your money
work for you?

So I'll get down upon my knees and bless the Working Man,
Who offers me a life of ease through all my mortal span;
Whose loins are lean to make me fat, who slaves to keep
me free,
Who dies before his prime to let me round the century;
Whose wife and children toil in turn until their strength
is spent,
That I may live in idleness upon my Five-per-Cent.
And if at times they curse me, why should I feel any blame?
For in my place I know that they would do the very same.
Aye, though they hoist a flag that's red on Sunday
afternoon,
Just offer them ten thousand pounds and see them change
their tune.
So I'll enjoy my dividends and live my life with zest,
And bless the mighty men who first—invented Interest.

ROBERT W. SERVICE

HYMN TO THE GLORY OF FREE ENTERPRISE

Solo: An Elder Statesman

1. Of freedom this and freedom that the drooling leftist chatters,
But freedom for Free Enterprise is all that really matters;
This freedom was ordained by God; upon it rest all others,
For man's divinest impulse is to over-reach his brothers;
And so to this celestial urge we make our offering votive;
Behind all human greatness lies the noble Profit Motive.

Chorus of Bankers, Brokers, Executives and Advertising Men

Then hail we now Free Enterprise,
Extol and give it praise!
In it the world's salvation lies,
Without it every freedom dies;
O glorious Free Enterprise—
The enterprise that pays!

Solo: The President of the Canadian Manufacturers' Association

2. For victory we're giving all, at scarcely more than cost,
But what's the good of victory if Free Enterprise is lost?
The war's demands for well-laid plans most loyally we've heeded,
But peace is quite a different thing—no planning then is needed.
So, while today these damned controls have stretched us on the rack,
The moment victory comes in sight we want our freedom back.

Chorus:

Then hail we now Free Enterprise,
Extol and give it praise!
In armed revolt we'll all arise
If any post-war party tries
To undermine Free Enterprise—
The enterprise that pays.

Solo: The President of the Canadian Bankers' Association

3. We face today a dreadful threat from fools who would destroy us;
   Of something called "Security" they prate in accents joyous.
   Security? Its cost alone would drive us to perdition;
   Besides, it kills initiative and suffocates ambition.
   Security breaks down the will, the urge that keeps men free,
   It stifles effort, starves the soul—except in men like me.

Chorus:

Then hail we now Free Enterprise,
Extol and give it praise!
While Marsh and Beveridge theorize,
Their deadly, bolshevistic lies
Are poisoning Free Enterprise—
The enterprise that pays.

Solo: The President of the Canadian Chamber of Commerce

4. At periods when Free Enterprise may not provide employment
   We dread the thought of hungry men—it lessens our enjoyment;
   The government must then step in, with this consideration:
   That any public works proposed do not increase taxation.
   Depressions, after all, my friends, much as we may deplore them,
   Are acts of God; who ever heard of blaming business for them?

Chorus:

Then hail we now Free Enterprise,
Extol and give it praise!
Of course, when profits shrink in size,
To lay men off is only wise;
We dearly love Free Enterprise—
But only when it pays.

Solo: The President of the Advertising Association

5. Conspirators on every side Free Enterprise have slandered,
Forgetting that it's given us the world's best living standard;
We eat and drink supremely well at Royal York and Rideau,
And no one drives more Cadillacs or bigger ones than we do.
How blind the socialist who plots this way of life to shatter!
Free Enterprise brings wealth to all—at least, to all who matter.

Chorus:

Then hail we now Free Enterprise,
Extol and give it praise!
The working man must recognize
That, if in want he lives and dies,
It's just his lack of enterprise—
The enterprise that pays!

Solo: The President of a Very, Very Large Corporation

6. Free Enterprise does not, of course, mean actual competition,
And cutting prices—God forbid! That's treason and sedition.
A "Gentlemen's Agreement" is the best of all devices
To stabilize our dividends, our markets, and our prices.
For taking risks we've little love; we set our whole affection
On something like monopoly, with adequate protection.

Chorus:

Then hail we now Free Enterprise,
Extol and give it praise!
In it the world's salvation lies,
Without it every freedom dies;
O glorious Free Enterprise,
O wonderful Free Enterprise,
O marvellous Free Enterprise—
The enterprise that pays!

J. D. KETCHUM

PANIC

There's panic in the papers
Stocks and bonds are cutting capers
Rich men jumping from skyscrapers.

What's the rumpus all about?
Peace broke out.

JOE WALLACE

FOR THE RECORD

I think that I live in a street
Where the evenings are decidedly darker,
A citizen of what is said to be a country,
In the year nineteen-sixty-four.

All the snow melts around April,
In August there is nothing to wait for,
The Fall is established in November,
January is mostly Winter.

A woman claims to be my wife
On the strength of which she lives in my house.
But I am also dangerous to some animals
And have at times been observed to eat them.

I have little to say about the structure of society,
There may be certain letters to write occasionally,
Certain amounts to pay when they become due,
But it is against the law for some people to hurt me.

In view of this I continue to lead
What I am told is an existence
Weeks ending in Sundays
Unasked questions scrupulously unanswered.

GEORGE JONAS

THE SERVICE CLUB

1

The Service Club, on Wednesday noons,
Put on their tags, and shouted tunes—
All songs of noble theme and style,
As, "Pack your troubles up and smile".

These "angels" never sang hosannas
But chanted, "We have no bananas."
The air was thick with "Bill" and "Jack",
And each man thumped the other's back.
A bowl of soup, a slab of beef
Went swiftly sliding down each throat:
Their mastication would bring grief
To ostrich, pelican or goat.
Then cigarettes came out to heal
All memories of their awful meal;
And some, to ease digestion's scars,
Smoked wheezy pipes and fat cigars;
For dinner at a service club
Is strong on smoke and short on grub.

2

The president then rapped a gong,
And chairs scraped back in raucous song;
And with a monumental boost
The speaker then was introduced.
And, when he started in to tell
Them only things they cared to hear,
Like blurring ghosts in cloudy hell
They gave him an attentive ear.
This famous orator was brought
Because he never dislodged thought.
And if the interest seemed to lag
He praised the clergy and the flag,
He lauded surgeons and their knives,
He blessed all mothers and all wives.

His talk was like a soothing drug
That made men want to kiss and hug;
Or give one hundred thousand bucks
To under-privileged woodchucks,
Who got this way, now here's the rub,
Because the motto of this club
Was ever this—the thought quite missed 'em—
That no one must destroy the System.

3

The speaker paused; he knew his speech
Had not disturbed a soul in reach;
And so he brought his gifts to rally
In one magnificent finale,
Wherein he spake, with raised hand:
"We live in God's anointed land,
The world is fine, the weather's grand!"
And at this most amazing truth
He took his chair and picked his tooth.
And all the ghosts in cloudy hell
Cried, "Bravo, bravo; all is well."
And when their wild applause had died
Men rushed in torrents to his side
And told how they were edified.

4

Next Wednesday noon, at half-past twelve,
These men to Barnum's Inn will go
To keep the vacuum of their days
In one sublime, perpetual flow.

WILSON MacDONALD

A PSALM OF MONTREAL

(The City of Montreal is one of the most rising and, in many respects, most agreeable on the American continent, but its inhabitants are as yet too busy with commerce to care greatly about the masterpieces of old Greek Art. In the Montreal Museum of Natural History I came upon two plaster casts, one of the Antinous and the other of the Discobolus—not the good one, but in my poem, of course, I intend the good one—banished from public view to a room where were all manner of skins, plants, snakes, insects, etc., and, in the middle of these, an old man stuffing an owl.

"Ah," said I, "so you have some antiques here; why don't you put them where people can see them?"

"Well, sir," answered the custodian, "you see they are rather vulgar."

He then talked a great deal and said his brother did all Mr. Spurgeon's printing.

The dialogue—perhaps true, perhaps imaginary, perhaps a little of the one and a little of the other—between the writer and this old man gave rise to the lines that follow:)

Stowed away in a Montreal lumber room
The Discobolus standeth and turneth his face to the wall;
Dusty, cobweb-covered, maimed and set at naught,
Beauty crieth in an attic and no man regardeth:
O God! O Montreal!

Beautiful by night and day, beautiful in summer and winter,
Whole or maimed, always and alike beautiful—
He preacheth gospel of grace to the skin of owls
And to one who seasoneth the skins of Canadian owls:
O God! O Montreal!

When I saw him I was wroth and I said, "O Discobolus!
Beautiful Discobolus, a Prince both among gods and men!
What doest thou here, how camest thou hither, Discobolus,
Preaching gospel in vain to the skins of owls?"
O God! O Montreal!

And I turned to the man of skins and said unto him, "O
thou man of skins,
Wherefore hast thou done thus to shame the beauty of the
Discobolus?"

But the Lord had hardened the heart of the man of skins
And he answered, "My brother-in-law is haberdasher to
    Mr. Spurgeon."
    O God! O Montreal!

"The Discobolus is put here because he is vulgar—
He has neither vest nor pants with which to cover his limbs;
I, Sir, am a person of most respectable connections—
My brother-in-law is haberdasher to Mr. Spurgeon."
    O God! O Montreal!

Then I said, "O brother-in-law to Mr. Spurgeon's
    haberdasher,
Who seasonest also the skins of Canadian owls,
Thou callest trousers 'pants', whereas I call them 'trousers',
Therefore thou art in hell-fire and may the Lord pity thee!"
    O God! O Montreal!

"Preferrest thou the gospel of Montreal to the gospel of
    Hellas,
The gospel of thy connection with Mr. Spurgeon's
    haberdashery to the gospel of the Discobolus?"
Yet none the less blasphemed he beauty saying, "The
    Discobolus hath no gospel,
But my brother-in-law is haberdasher to Mr. Spurgeon."
    O God! O Montreal!

SAMUEL BUTLER

THE FOOTBALL MATCH

I

O wild kaleidoscopic panorama of jaculatory arms and legs.
The twisting, twining, turning, tussling, throwing, thrusting,
    throttling, tugging, thumping, the tightening thews.
The tearing of tangled trousers, the jut of giant calves protuberant.
The wriggleness, the wormlike, snaky movement and life of it;

The insertion of strong men in the mud, the wallowing, the stamping with thick shoes;
The rowdyism, and *élan*, the slugging and scraping, the cowboy Homeric ferocity.
(Ah, well kicked, red legs! Hit her up, you muddy little hero, you!)
The bleeding noses, the shins, the knuckles abraded:
That's the way to make men! Go it, you border ruffians, I like ye.

II

Only two sorts of men are any good, I wouldn't give a cotton hat for no other—
The Poet and the Plug Ugly. They are picturesque. Oh, but ain't they?
These college chaps, these bouncing fighters from M'Gill and Toronto,
Are all right. I must have a fighter, a bully, somewhat of a desperado;
Of course, I prefer them raw, uneducated, unspoiled by book rot;
I reckon these young fellows, these howling Kickapoos of the puddle, these boys,
Have been uneducated to an undemocratic and feudal-aristocratic extent;
Lord! how they can kick, though! Another man slugged there!

III

Unnumbered festoons of pretty Canadian girls, I salute you;
Howl away, you non-playing encouragers of the kickers!
Rah, Rah, Rah, Rah, Rah, Rah, M'Gill!
Rah, Rah, Rah, Sis, Boom, Toronto! Lusty-throated give it!
Oh, wild, tumultuous, multitudinous shindy. Well, this *is* the boss;
This is worth coming twenty miles to see. Personally, I haven't had so much fun since I was vaccinated.
I wonder if the Doctor spectates it. Here is something beyond his plesiosauri.

Purely physical glow and exultation this of abundantest muscle:
I wish John Sullivan were here.

IV

Oh, the kicking, stamping, punching, the gore and the glory of battle!
Kick, kick, kick, kick, kick, kick. *Will* you kick!
You kickers, scoop up the mud, steam plough the field,
Fall all over yourselves, squirm out! Look at that pile-driver of a full-back there!
Run, leg it, hang on to the ball; say, you big chump, don't you kill that little chap
When you are about it.
Well, I'd like to know what a touchdown is, then? Draw?
Where's your draw?
Yer lie!

ANON.

THE CANADIAN SOCIAL REGISTER

(A Social Register for Canada was promoted in Montreal in 1947. On the Advisory Committee were names like Rt. Hon. Louis St. Laurent, Sir Ellsworth Flavelle, Air-Marshal Bishop, Rear-Admiral Brodeur, Hon. J. Earl Lawson, Hartland Molson, and others. A Secret Committee was to screen all applicants. All quotations in this poem are taken verbatim from the invitation sent out to prospective members.)

Reader, we have the honour to invite you to become a "Member of the Social Register",
For the paltry fee of $125 per annum.
This "work of art, done in good taste", and listing annually the "Notables of the Dominion",
Will contain nothing but "Ladies and Gentlemen pre-eminent in the Higher Spheres",
A list, indeed, of "First Families",
Who are "the very fabric of our country".
Thus shall we "build up in the Nation's First Families
A consciousness of their rôle in the life of a civilized democracy".

Thus shall we bring "added dignity and profound significance
To our cultural way of life".
Through deplorable lack of vision, in times past,
Men who were "great Canadians, have everlastingly passed into oblivion",
Leaving no "footprints on the sands of time".
Somehow, despite their pre-eminence, they have disappeared.
Shall we, through "tragic shortsightedness", let the leaders of this era
"Disappear into the realm of eternal silence"?
"Shall there be no names, no achievements, to hearten and strengthen on-coming generations in time of stress"?
If they have failed to make history, shall they fail to make The Canadian Social Register?
No—not if they can pay $125 annually,
And pass our Secret Committee.
For there is a "Secret Committee of seven members",
Who will "determine the eligibility of those applying for membership".
Thus will the Social Register be "accepted in the most fastidious circles".
And to aid the Secret Committee you will send
The name of your father and the maiden name of your mother,
And the address of your "summer residence",
(For of course you have a summer residence).
You may also submit, with a glossy print of yourself,
"Short quotations from laudatory comments received on diverse public occasions".
When printed, the Register will be sent,
Free, gratis, and not even asked for,
To (among many others) the "King of Sweden", the "President of Guatemala", and the "Turkish Public Library".

Reader, this will be a "perennial reminder"
Of the people (or such of them as pass the Secret Committee)
Who "fashioned this Canada of ours",
For "One does not live only for toil and gain",
Not, anyway, in First Families. It is comforting to believe

That while we "walk the earth", and pay $125,
And "after we have passed on", there will remain
"In the literature of the Universe", and particularly in the "Turkish Public Library",
This "de luxe edition", "these unique and dignified annals",
"These priceless and undying memories", with laudatory comments chosen by ourselves,
To which "succeeding First Families and historians alike will look",
For "knowledge, guidance and inspiration".
Lives rich in eligibility will be "written large",
(But within "a maximum of one thousand words")
"For all men to see and judge".
The "glorious dead", too,
These "selfless and noble defenders of Canada's honour",
Will be incorporated in the Social Register
"Without any financial remuneration",
Assuming, of course, that they are all
"Sons and daughters of its Members".

Reader, as you may guess, the Register
Was not "a spur of the moment idea".
It was "long and carefully nurtured",
And "counsel was sought in high and authoritative places",
So that it may "lay a basis upon which prominent Canadians will henceforth be appraised
As they go striding down the years",
Paying their $125,
And receiving a "world-wide, gratuitous distribution",
Even unto "the Turkish Public Library".

"Si monumentum requiris, circumspice!"
On this note, we both end.

F. R. SCOTT

LISTED

The neurotic bed, the psychopathic stove,
The partisan party-line, the reluctant boat,
The detective draught, the reach of radio-love,
The invisible tool and the unquotable thought,

The effusive ice-box and the elusive ice,
The evasive cockroach and the pervasive ant,
The incisive squirrel and the invasive mice,
The derisive wasp and the abusive bent,

The partial partition and the cringing hinge,
The pump that will not and the leak that will,
The dubious odour, the suspicious tinge,
The weight outwitting, twitting the muscles' skill,

The maze of menus, the deadline for supplies,
The dervish dishes, the hot-cold and cold-hot,
The clacks of swatters and the cliques of flies,
The clock that is read, the volume that is not,

The scurrilous hornet, querulous mosquito,
Misplaced toad, bat, skunk, porcupine and snake,
And the storm that, when for once in a way one could see to
Look, rips the invitation of the lake.

ROBERT FINCH

SATURDAY SUNDAE

The triple-decker and the double-cone
I side-swipe swiftly, suck the coke-straws dry,
Ride toadstool seat beside the slab of morgue—
Sweet corner drug-store, sweet pie in the sky.

Him of the front-flap apron, him I sing,
The counter-clockwise clerk in underalls.
Swing low, sweet chocolate, Oh swing, swing,
While cheek by juke the jitter chatter falls.

I swivel on my axle and survey
The latex tintex kotex cutex land.
Soft kingdoms sell for dimes, *Life Pic Look Click*
Inflate the male with conquest girly grand.

My brothers and my sisters, two by two,
Sit sipping succulence and sighing sex.
Each tiny adolescent universe
A world the vested interests annex.

Such bread and circuses these times allow,
Opium most popular, life so small and slick.
Perhaps with candy is the new world born
And cellophane shall wrap the heretic.

F. R. SCOTT

THE PENGUIN

Penguin, penguin comme il faut
Amid Antarctic ice and snow
Tell us what divine decree
Ordains thy strict formality?

What occasion, what affair
Prescribes a dress so debonair?
To what revels dost thou go
With front immaculate as snow?

Bird of contradictious hue
Tell us, penguin, what or who
Entertains this frozen coast:
What dread party? what dread Host?

Penguin, what should I conclude
From thy solemn attitude?
From thy decent gravity
What lesson? Penguin . . . Can it be?

He who made me what I am
Who clad the tiger and the lamb—
God, from whom all dressing flows,
Sets the fashion of thy clothes.

Penguin, Hail! Beyond a doubt
Not gay, but decently devout:
Abide with us till God on high
Requests our company (white tie).

MICHAEL HORNYANSKY

HOW BLACK WAS MY CADILLAC

(SUMMIT CIRCLE, WESTMOUNT MOUNTAIN)

May is a Jovial month,
father of inviolate violets
that on Summit Circle peep
fearfully at the grisly
intruders who have woodenly
-and-concretely formed
ranks to do battle with
the green things.

Frost is a friendly saboteur
and the violets nod to the
wind exultantly as they
watch Norma Shearer's mouldered
error in adobe shuddering from
the ravages of its latest
winter, suffering from fallen
red tiles and rent walls.

Paint is a reactionary ally
to the older fighters, and
the Timmins' mansion, a
reclusive giant fighting
a drowsy rearguard action,
takes on new colour,
lies about its age and
stands its decaying ground.

But construction is the cruel foe
that frightens the flowers
and threatens to lay them all
waste with wanton contempt;
free-form comedians caper
into position on the western
perimeter, leering drunkenly
at the helpless greenery.

The green things count
their dead: half an acre
of white birch on the
northern slope, sagging

under a winter's weight
of snow-dumped cinders;
five acres of grass, fern
and buttercups obliterated
by Comedians' Row.

Sunday is a quiet time,
unreal to the green
things; and the
dandelions
stare blankly at an
orange bulldozer
dozing
in the sun.

ROBERT A. CURRIE

GOLFERS

Like Sieur Montaigne's distinction
between virtue and innocence
what gets you is their unbewilderment

They come into the picture suddenly
like unfinished houses, gaps and planed wood,
dominating a landscape

And you see at a glance
among sportsmen they are the metaphysicians,
intent, untalkative, pursuing Unity

(What finally gets you is their chastity)

And that no theory of pessimism is complete
which altogether ignores them

IRVING LAYTON

THE LIFELESS WIFE

The lifeless wife
Kisses with pursed lips
Her grim husband (thin
Pinstriped businessman);
She is his safe
Deposit box and bank,
The nickelodeon
That plays his favourite tune.

She was just an ordinary
Woman: all he had to do
To make her fully his
In pure domestic bliss

Was just break through
Her backbone, empty out her head,
Stuff her heart with money
And bury her in bed.

MARGARET ATWOOD

SINALÓA

Si, señor, is halligators here, your guidebook say it,
si, jaguar in the montanas, maybe helephants, quien sabe?
You like, those palm trees in the sunset? Certamente very nice,
it happen each night in the guide tourista.
But who the hell eat jaguar, halligator, you heat them?
Mira my fren, wat this town need is muy big breakwater—
  I like take hax to them jeezly palmas,

So you want to buy machete? Por favor, I give you
sousand machete you give me one grand bulldozer, hey?
Wat this country is lack, señor, is real good goosin,
is need pinehapple shove hup her bottom
(sure, sure, is bella all those water-ayacints)
is need drains for sugarcane in them pittoresca swamps—
  and shoot all them anarquista egrets.

Hokay, you like bugambilla, ow you say, flower-hung cliffs?
Is how old, the Fort? Is Colhuan, muy viejo, before Moses, no?
Is for you, señor, take em away, send us helevator for weat.
It like me to see all them fine boxcar stuff full rice,
sugar, flax, all rollin down to those palmstudded ports
were Cortez and all that crap (you heat history?)—
  and bugger the pink flamingos.

Amigo, we make you present all them two-weel hoxcart,
you send em Quebec, were my brudder was learn to be padre,
wc takc ditchdiggcrs, tractors, Massey-Arris yes?
Sinalóa want ten sousand mile irrigation canals,
absolutamente. Is fun all that organ-cactus fence?
Is for the birds, señor; is more better barbwire, verdad?—
  and chingar those cute little burros.

Sin argumento, my fren, is a beautiful music,
all them birds. Pero, wy you no like to hear combos,
refrigerator trucks? Is wonderful on straight new ighway,
jampack with melons, peppers, bananas, tomatoes, si, si . . .
Chirrimoyas? Mangos? You like! Is for Indios, solamente,
is bruise, no can ship, is no bueno, believe me, señor—
  and defecar on those goddam guidebook.

EARLE BIRNEY

ANGLOSAXON STREET

Dawndrizzle ended,   dampness steams from
blotching brick and   blank plasterwaste.
Faded housepatterns,   hoary and finicky,
unfold stuttering,   stick like a phonograph.
Over the eaves and   over dank roofs
peep giraffetowers,   pasted planless
against grey sky,   great dronecliffs
like cutouts for kids,   clipped in two dimensions . . .

Here is a ghetto   gotten for goyim,
O with care denuded   of nigger and kike.
No coonsmell rankles,   reeks only cellarrot,
attar of carexhaust,   catcorpse and cookinggrease.
Imperial hearts   heave in this haven.
Cracks across windows   are welded with slogans;
There'll Always Be An England   enhances geraniums,
and V's for a *Victory*   vanquish the housefly.

Ho! with climbing sun,   heading from cocoons,
go bleached beldames,   garnished in bargainbasements,
festooned with shoppingbags,   farded, flatarched,
bigthewed Saxonwives,   stepping over buttrivers,
waddling back to suckle   smallfry, wienerladen.

Hoy! with sunslope,   shrieking over hydrants,
flood from learninghall   the lean fingerlings,
Nordic, nobblecheeked,   not all clean of nose,
leaping Commando-wise   into leprous lanes.

What! after whistleblow   spewed from wheelboat,
after daylong doughtiness,   dire handplay
in sewertrench or sandpit,   come Saxonthegns,
Junebrown Jutekings,   jawslack for meat.

Sit after supper   on smeared doorsteps
not humbly swearing   hatedeeds on Huns,
profiteers, politicians,   pacifists and Jews.

Then by twobit magic   to muse in movie,
unlock picturehoard,   or lope to alehall,
soaking bleakly   in beer, skittleless.

Home again to hotbox   and humid husbandhood,
in slumbertrough adding   sleepily to Anglekin.
Alongside in lanenooks   carling and leman
caterwaul and clip,   careless of Saxonry,
with moonglow and haste   and a higher heartbeat.

Slumbers now slumtrack,   unstinks, cooling,
waiting brief for milkhind,   mornstar and worldrise.

EARLE BIRNEY

ANGLO-CANADIAN

A native of Kingston, Ont.
—two grandparents Canadian
and still living

His complexion florid
as a maple leaf in late autumn,
for three years he attended
Oxford

Now his accent
makes even Englishmen
wince, and feel
unspeakably colonial.

IRVING LAYTON

ON THE APPOINTMENT OF GOVERNOR-GENERAL VINCENT MASSEY, 1952

Let the Old World, where rank's yet vital,
Part those who have and have not title.
Toronto has no social classes—
Only the Masseys and the masses.

B. K. SANDWELL

THE CALL OF THE WILD

Make me over, Mother Nature,
Take the knowledge from my eyes,
Put me back among the pine trees
Where the simple are the wise.

Clear away all evil influence
That can hurt me from the States.
Keep me pure among the beaver
With un-Freudian loves and hates,

Where my Conrads are not Aiken
Where John Bishop's Peales don't sound,
Where the Ransoms are not Crowing
And the Ezras do not Pound.

F. R. SCOTT

FESTIVAL AT STRATFORD

Here where the swans are,
fanfares flourish, princes
parley, togas swirl,
and in the long motels

later lie lovers
fervid for fulness,
swans fed, drama
done, towelled dry,

whiskey aside, jesters
remembered, sorrow
madness, roads unmoving,
night's kiss to come.

PETER MILLER

LEDA IN STRATFORD, ONT.

A silly country maiden went
A mile or so to Stratford, Ont.,
And here she found, as everywhere,
Things much too ordin'ry for her;
Yet from a Richard, Rex, or clown
She learned of Leda and the Swan,
And so admired their high-class union
That up and down the banks of Avon
She ogled those immaculate birds
That never turned to take her crumb
Or listen to her honeyed words
Of love, but simply swam.

A crow, observing her odd wish,
Laid the girl beneath a bush;
No sudden blow—the great wings beating—
More as a joke, a kind of larking.
And yet she doted on his action,
Tickled by such rare seduction,
Boasting to the birds, "Black Swan,
Demon Lover urged me on."
But no bird listened, for a caw,
Loud and rude, came from the crow.

ANNE WILKINSON

ODE TO FREDERICTON

White are your house-tops, white too your vaulted elms
That make your stately streets long aisles of prayer,
And white your thirteen spires that point your God
Who reigns afar in pure and whiter air,
And white the dome of our democracy—
The snow has pitied you and made you fair,
O snow-washed city of cold, white Christians,
So white you will not cut a black man's hair.

FRED COGSWELL

FREDERICTON

So this is "the poets' corner
Of Canada"—Bliss, Sir Charles,
And Francis Joseph Sherman,
All born, all Latin'd and Greek'd here.

Not one of them
With anything really to say,
But dressing it up, faking it,
So that they fooled quite a few in their time.

And I can understand why.
Outside of the noble river
Which none of them bothered to write about,
This city has little to commend it,
And couldn't help but in time
Drive a man to drink or lousy poetry.
Which vices are no doubt being practised
By their loyal torchbearers today.

RAYMOND SOUSTER

LOCAL BOY

His father having uttered the proper words in the proper places;
The post-Varsity period of yellow roadsters, champagne and chorus girls
Having ended in one monster hangover too many;
The abortionist having been paid off by the family lawyer,
And the broken mis-engagement settled by proxy,
He could now take his place, aged twenty-nine,
As private secretary to the managing director,
With a suitable desk of his own, as his father's heir.
Green light all the way; the pre-ordained marriage assured
To the daughter of father's old friend,
(When the merger went through, of course—no point in a public offering of shares).

A year abroad, with the crest of the honeymoon in Italy,
Unmarred by stray and ugly sprouts of neglected wild oats.
Visits to the foreign branches, as a matter of routine,
("Good to get to know the people I'll have to rely on.")
Three children, a place in the country, voting stock on the
    board,
With the chairmanship inevitable.
No one could doubt that a seat in the Senate awaited him
When the distinguishing touch of the grey appeared at the
    temples.

VERNAL HOUSE

SOUVENIRS DU TEMPS PERDU

(For LEON EDEL)

The champignon salad has repeated
to the verge of tedium.
We sit in the Dôme
to the ditto of le même
as French as a french fried potato
in a greasy cornucopia
of the *Montreal Daily Star*.
I will arise and go now
and go to the lavabo
where men without women
are standing in a row.
  Don John of Austria
  has doffed his winter drawers
  Don John of Austria
  is riding with the whores.
God I will rise and take a train
and get me to April once again
for April is the cruellest nymph
scattering garters and spent stays
on an unmade bed in a one-room head.
  Oh to be in April now that
  yes sir she's my baby . . .

Would you mind not forgetting
to leave something in the bowl
as you
pass out.

A. J. M. SMITH

LANDLADY

Through sepia air the boarders come and go,
impersonal as trains. Pass silently
the craving silence swallowing her speech;
click doors like shutters on her camera eye.

Because of her their lives become exact:
their entrances and exits are designed;
phone calls are cryptic. Oh, her ticklish ears
advance and fall back stunned.

Nothing is unprepared. They hold the walls
about them when they weep or laugh. Each face
is dialled to zero publicly. She peers
stippled with curious flesh;

pads on the patient landing like a pulse,
unlocks their keyholes with the wire of sight,
searches their rooms for clues when they are out,
pricks when they come home late.

Wonders when they are quiet, jumps when they move,
dreams that they dope or drink, trembles to know
the traffic of their brains, jaywalks their street
in clumsy shoes.

Yet knows them better than their closest friends:
their cupboards and the secrets of their drawers,
their books, their private mail, their photographs
are theirs and hers.

Knows when they wash, how frequently their clothes
go to the cleaners, what they like to eat,
their curvature of health, but even so
is not content.

For, like a lover, must know all, all, all.
Prays she may catch them unprepared at last
and palm the dreadful riddle of their skulls—
hoping the worst.

P. K. PAGE

FUNERAL OF AN ADMINISTRATOR

Build high the mound and pyre;
Let the flame fling its glory,
Roll its convolving flower,
Bower soul in that bright eyrie.

Swing the loud bell a-tolling,
Rolling billow higher
(Cumulus unseen piling)
To where the angels tower

To lift the proud soul softly
Up through the skies all argent,
Then with superb wings deftly
Heave it to where the cogent

City's eternal circle
Rests on secure foundation
Guarded by sword of Michael
And St. Paul's assertion.

Speak of the wolf no evil,
Bury him in sheep's clothing,
Shoulder your axe and shovel
And go home, saying nothing.

ROY DANIELLS

THE CONVICT HOLOCAUST

(Columbus, Ohio, 1930)

Waiting their turn to be identified,
After their fiery contact with the walls,
Three hundred pariahs ranged side by side
Upon the floors along the cattle stalls!

The fires consumed their numbers with their breath,
Charred out their names; though many of the dead
Gave proof of valour, just before their death,
That Caesar's legions might have coveted.

But these, still subject to the law's commands,
Received the last insignia of the cell:
The guards went through them, straightened out their hands,
And with the ink-brush got the thumb-prints well.

E. J. PRATT

THE HANGING

"It has been decided that the law must be allowed to take its course."

DAILY PAPER

THE LAW SPEAKS:

I bind the Soul that fathered me;
I am the Law, and resolute
Against the growing of the Soul,
I hang, behead, electrocute.

I take my course. How fine the day!
And all are here by duty stirred,
Hangman and prisoner, warden and press,
And Jesus with the Holy Word.

I am the Law. May order rule!
My warrant let the warden read,
Then all with proper decency
Will to our lifted stage proceed.

How fine the day! The happy sun
Beams into corridor and square
To cheer our prisoner and bless
The purpose of our altar there.

Our footsteps on the sunny stones
Beat to the pulse of earth and star;
The law that drives yon budding tree
Condemned our prisoner at its bar.

Let Jesus hold his trembling arm
And stand beside him to the end
(He loves these opportunities
To function as experienced friend).

Now, hangman, use your cunning well,
And hide his face that none may see
The anguish of his tortured soul.
I take my course, let these things be.

Come, Jesus, speak your little prayer
And, when "Deliver us" is said,
Then, hangman, draw the gliding bolt
And give our brother air to tread.

"Our Father," sound the gracious words,
"Thy will be done"—and all the rest—
(I hope our poor delivered friend
Had time to note the subtle jest).

He shoots into the open dark,
His soul is torn through narrow ways.
I take my course. I only see
A straightened rope that trembling sways.

I bind the Soul that fathered me;
I am the Law, and resolute
Against the growing of the Soul,
I hang, behead, electrocute.

J. E. H. MacDONALD

IV.
SNOW, DUST, HAIL AND RUST

WINTER IN LOWER CANADA

Thou barren waste; unprofitable strand,
Where hemlocks brood on unproductive land,
Whose frozen air on one bleak winter's night
Can metamorphose *dark brown hares to white*!

Here forests crowd, unprofitable lumber,
O'er fruitless lands indefinite as number;
Where birds scarce light, and with the north winds veer
On wings of wind, and quickly disappear.
Here the rough Bear subsists his winter year,
And licks his paw and finds *no better fare*. . . .

One month we hear birds, shrill and loud and harsh,
The plaintive bittern sounding from the marsh;
The next we see the fleet-winged swallow,
The duck, the woodcock, and the ice-birds follow;
Then comes drear clime, the lakes all stagnant grow,
And the wild wilderness is rapt in snow.

The lank Canadian eager trims his fire,
And all around their simpering stoves retire;
With fur-clad friends their progenies abound,
And thus regale their buffaloes around;
Unlettered race, how few the number tells,
Their only pride a *cariole and bells*!
To mirth or mourning, thus by folly led,
To mix in pleasure or to chaunt the dead!
To seek the chapel prostrate to adore,
Or leave their fathers' coffins at the door!
Perchance they revel; still around they creep,
And talk, and smoke, and spit, and drink, and sleep!

STANDISH O'GRADY

THE BACHELOR IN HIS SHANTY

'Tis something strange a chiel like me
Should frae his native country flee,
And leave his freens o' social glee—
    And loves sae dear,
And cross the braid Atlantic sea
    In quest o' gear.

To come to this strange land o' trees,
The vile abode o' frogs and fleas,
Wi' no ane near to sympatheese,
    Or yet to hate us;
Devour'd alive by slow degrees
    By curs'd mosquitoes. . . .

Roasted by the summer's heat—
Till life's weak pulse can scarcely beat,
Half drown'd in streams o' creeshy sweat
    That gem my beard,
As thick as morning's dewy weet,
    On flow'ry sward.

Followed by Winter's biting breeze,
That tears the mantle off the trees,
Nips a' the flow'rs, kills a' the bees
    Wi' savage sway;
And ilka birdie frightened flees,
    To the south away. . . .

When storms are o'er we look for calms,
And sae did I midst a' my dwams,
Yet e'en last nicht while Hope's sweet balms
    Cur'd every sore,
The wolves commenc'd their eldrich psalms
    At my very door.

Their music I was doom'd to hear,
Though far frae pleasant to the ear;

But waur than that, twa lambs sae dear,
And baith their mithers,
Were aff next morn, I ne'er ken'd where,
Tail, head, and shouthers!

A grumphy, too, I fed with care,
Till he might weigh twal' stane or mair;
And when about to scrape his hair,
Though no' that able,
A muckle black and ugly bear
Saved me the trouble.

Hens, ducks and geese, a motley group,
Were carried off at ae fell swoop;
Nae wonder that my spirits droop,
And heart turns sair,
And sunk ayont a' earthly hope
In fell despair.

A farmer too I'm called by name,
Nay—even a Laird—so much for fame,
Which makes me blush wi' burnin' shame
The truth to tell,
For a' my craps scarce fill my wame
And nane to sell.

Twa-three bits o' potato hills,
For stumps are sworn foes to drills,
Some pumpkins big as cadger's creels,
Is a' my crop;
For aught I raise, markets and mills
Might a' gie up. . . .

The crickets squeak like sucking pigs,
And dance about my fire their jigs,
Syne eat my stockings, feet and legs,
The hungry deevils;
Sure Egypt e'en wi' a' her plagues
Had ne'er sic evils.

Oh! had I but some sonsy quean,
To keep me warm and keep me clean,
I would not care the frosts a preen,
Nor heats nor agues;
But then to court ane beats me clean
And that the plague is.

Last week my humble suit I paid
To bonnie, smirking Maggie Shade;
She seem'd to list to what I said,
But mark, ye fates,
Straightway wi' guessing Sam she fled
Aff to the States.

ROBERT BOYD

ANNANDALE FARMING

Please read the pleasures of a Farmer's life,
Arranged and class'd in this sage document.
Dead sheep, daft bargains, a tea-drinking wife;
Dull markets, partial payments, a long rent;
Debts and a purse (but here begins a strife
'Tween my twa keekers which shall most lament
Their owner's fortunes; well, I say a purse),
Smit with consumption, weak, and getting worse.

Four or five horses, leaning 'gainst their stalls,
Eight calvers, high of bone and hard of skin;
Some forty porkers, making hideous squawls,
Through lack of murphies pitifully thin,
With savage snouts they undermine the walls;
Soon shall the half-rotten roof-tree tumble in
And crack their rigbones, pound their hams and fletches,
And put a finisher upon the wretches. . . .

Ye happy few, ye owners of the soil,
Who feed upon the fat and drink the sweet,
Just look and see how your poor tenants toil,
And after a' have hardly bread to eat:
Let down your rents, live and let live the while,
And we will be your servants, as 'tis meet;
We'll gang and buy ourselves new coats and breeks,
And never speak a word on politics.

ALEX. GLENDINNING

From EPISTLE TO HUGH M'DONALD, ESQ., GLASGOW

Now, in this God-forgotten land,
Upon my lonely isle I stand,
And view the far-receding strand
O' Fundy's bay,
Without one object, rich or grand,
To fire my lay.

O, lack-a-day! my dainty Hugh,
This country's no for me nor you—
A bleak, bare wilderness a' through,
I dare be sworn,
Nor laverock springing frae the dew
To wake the morn.

Nae heather here waives on the knowes,
Nae gowden broom in beauty grows,
Nae bearded thistle bauldly rows
Its tassels free,
Nor blinkin' gowan decks the howes
Wi' laughing e'e.

The sheep and kye, on hill and plain,
Are dwarfish heaps o' skin and bane—
The pigs alone can fatness gain
On this damned soil,

Whaur worms can scantly creep their lane
For lack o' chyle.

For five lang months stern winter reigns
Despotic o'er these wide domains;
His icy spear makes hills and plains
His vengeance share,
With lakes and rivers bound by chains
Fast to their lair.

Soon as December, dark and drear,
Brings Christmas sports and dinners near,
Ere yet auld Scotia's blythe new year
Is welcom'd ben,
His biting winds and snaws appear
Frae's norlan' den.

And, Lord, when ance they hae begun,
Drift after drift comes wi' the win',
Till syne when ance their race is run
And spent their might
Three feet o' snaw hides mother grun'
Frae mortal sight.

God pity, then, the poor blue-noses,
Their cheeks like flour, their nebs like roses;
They puff, they grue, and swallow doses
To heat their wame,
Till aft when night their business closes
They hiccup hame.

Partridge Island
Saint John, N.B.
April 1st, 1856

WILLIAM MURDOCK

OLD NICK IN SOREL

Old Nick took a fancy, as many men tell,
To come for a winter to live in Sorel.
Yet the snow fell so deep as he came in his sleigh,
That his fingers and toes were frost-nipt on the way.

In truth, said the demon, who'd ever suppose,
I must go back again with the loss of all those;
In either extreme, sure it matters me not,
If I freeze upon earth or at home I'm too hot;

So he put back his sleigh, for he thought it amiss,
His clime to compare to a climate like this;
And now 'tis resolved that this frightful new-comer
Will winter in hell and be here in the summer.

STANDISH O'GRADY

RURAL HENHOUSE

A stink assails the nostrils delicately
        #2 twists and avoids the hatchery
                401 sails serenely on
                        laid out by a Roman drunk no doubt—

Here on rural highway 28 (dirt with
gravel under)
                        potholes like catastrophes
(negotiable by Ford
                                Chevy
                                        and Plymouth)
Plymouth Rocks assert supremacy
challenged only by Buff Orpington
and white Leghorns in these green dominions
of vanquished hawks and lost
territorial domain
of weasels duped electrically
and rats dispatched by science
    these call girls coaxed
    by kilowatts' chicanery
    to lay for more than 24 hours—

Apart
from world's public incubator
(that giant kennel)
this
unscrubbed unsterile uterus uprears
unpainted boards in a barnyard nook
and "who pecks whom?" is
the battle cry while
Pithecanthropus Erectus round
the kitchen midden peers
disguised as Homo Sapiens he
asserts his own supremacy
with registered cows and A.I.D.
worships new fertility gods
delicious ground cantharides
assures a profit from a loss—
The mommas stalk like Caesar's wives
across the barnyard
brown mothers
redcap roosters
new-born chicks
chirruping yellow powder puffs
(O pterodactyl's child)
quis custodiet of the green morning
ecce homo in the family widdershins who
is viable but unattractive
the farmer
secretive
close-hinged
essays for all of us including him a
proper honest and agrarian smile—

And
in those far away high-climbing ice-blue cities
in warmed over fourth floor apartments
distant semi-detached villas
chill duplex bungalows
frowning tenants
eye hungrily

orange embryos on porcelain and blue tables those
boiled elliptical billiard balls skittishly
rolling into
                penultimate eggcups—

Some inner part of you and me awaits helplessly
(along with
                somehow
                                misunderstood and ludicrous
all originally clean things
come loitering in across the sun's white tablecloth)
                uneasily our bound and gagged selves
await like catatonics the
                abrupt and violating spoon—

Let us eat now—

ALFRED PURDY

SONG TO THE FOUR SEASONS

Spring is here, the breezes blowing,
Four inches of top-soil going, going;
Farm ducks rolling across the prairie;
Spring is here—how nice and airy!

Summer has come, the hoppers are back,
The sun shines bright, the fields shine black,
Cloudlets gather, it looks like rain—
Ah, the patter of hail on the window-pane!

Bounteous harvest, we'll sell at cost—
To-morrow we'll have an early frost:
Glorious autumn, red with rust;
We'll live on the general store on trust.

A long, quiet winter with plenty of snow,
And plenty of barley; it's eighty below,
Barley in the heater, salt pork in the pantry—
How nice that you never feel cold in this country.

P. G. HIEBERT

MANITOBA BECOMES A PROVINCE

August 15, 1870

Now everybody, drunk or sober,
Sing loud the praise of Manitoba;
Throw back your head, inflate your chest,
And sing the glories of the West;
Sing, without slackening or stop,
The jubilation of the crop;
Sing of the bending ear of wheat,
That stands at least some fourteen feet;
And soft its tasselled head inclines,
To flirt with the potato vines;
Sing of the prairie covered over,
With cabbage trees and shrubs of clover;
While English settlers lose their way,
In forests of gigantic hay.
  How wonderful be it confessed,
  The passing of the by-gone West;
The painted Indian rides no more,
He stands—at a tobacco store;
His cruel face proclaims afar
The terror of the cheap cigar;
Behold his once down-trodden squaw,
Protected by Provincial Law;
Their tee-pee has become—Oh, gee,
A station on the G.T.P.,
And on the scenes of Ancient War,
Thy rails I.C.O.C.P.R.

STEPHEN LEACOCK

THE FARMER AND THE FARMER'S WIFE

The farmer and the farmer's wife
Lead frolicsome and carefree lives,
And all their work is but in play,
Their labours only exercise.

The farmer leaps from bed to board,
And board to binder on the land;
His wife awakes with shouts of joy,
And milks a cow with either hand.

Then all in fun they feed the pigs,
And plough the soil in reckless glee,
And play the quaint old-fashioned game
Of mortgagor and mortgagee.

And all day long they dash about,
In barn and pasture, field and heath;
He sings a merry roundelay,
She whistles gaily through her teeth.

And when at night the chores are done,
And hand in hand they sit and beam,
He helps himself to applejack,
And she to Paris Green.

P. G. HIEBERT

TO MY FATHER, JACOB BINKS

I used to think the cut-worm and the weevil,
Were things that blindly come and go by chance,
And Hessian-fly an undiluted evil,
To make the farmer shudder in his pants;

But now I know they hold him to his acre,
For could he ever win and take his ease,
He'd up and leave his binder and his breaker,
And give the precious land back to the Crees.

I used to think the beetle and the hopper
Were but a pest, but now I realize
That French-weed as a yield is right and proper,
And cut-worms are a blessing in disguise;

That rust, and hail, and stem-rot are protection,
And what we call the drought year is a means
To keep the farmer on his quarter section,
Although it makes him tremble in his jeans.

The things that we call trials are a warning,
The thing we call the gopher is a boon,
For should a crop appear some early morning,
The farmer would be gone by afternoon;

The hopper should be cherished and be shielded,
And Hessian-fly is something we should trust—
If what we call the crop is ever yielded,
You'll never see the farmer for his dust.

P. G. HIEBERT

PRAIRIE GRAVEYARD

Wind mutters thinly on the sagging wire
binding the graveyard from the gouged dirt road,
bends thick-bristled Russian thistle,
sifts listless dust
into cracks in hard grey ground.
Empty prairie slides away
on all sides, rushes toward a wide
expressionless horizon, joined
to a vast blank sky.

Lots near the road are the most expensive
where heavy tombstones lurch a fraction
tipped by splitting soil.
Farther, a row of aimless heaps
names weather-worn from tumbled sticks
remember now the six thin children
of a thin, shiftless home.

Hawk, wind-scouring, cuts
a pointed shadow on the drab scant grass.

Two graves apart by the far fence
are suicides, one with a grand
defiant tombstone, bruising at the heart
"Death is swallowed up in victory".
(And may be, God's kindness being more large
than man's, to this, who after seven years
of drought, burned down his barn,
himself hanged in it.)
The second, nameless, set around
with even care-sought stones
(no stones on this section)
topped with two plants, hard-dried,
in rust-thick jam tins in the caked drab pile,

A gopher jumps from a round cave,
springs furtively, spurts under fence, is gone.

Wind raises dead curls of dust and whines
under its harsh breath on the limp dragged wires,
then leaves the graveyard stiff with silence, lone
in the centre of the huge lone land and sky.

ANNE MARRIOTT

ESTEVAN, SASKATCHEWAN

A small town bears the mark of Cain,
Or the oldest brother with the dead king's wife
In a foul relation as viewed by sons,
Lies on the land, squat, producing
Love's queer offspring only,
Which issue drives the young
To feign a summer madness, consort with skulls,
While the farmer's chorus, a Greek harbinger,
Forecasts by frost or rings about the moon
How ill and black the seeds will grow.

This goodly frame, the earth, each of its sons,
With nature as a text, and common theme
The death of fathers, anguished in betrayal
From the first family returns a sacrifice
Of blood's brother, a splintered eyeball
Groined in the fields, scarecrow to crows.
This warns Ophelia to her morning song,
Bawdy as a lyric in a pretty brain gone bad,
While on those fields the stupid harvest lies.

E. W. MANDEL

BACKGROUND

Where I come from, the kick of love
recalls the laughter in the throats
of boys who knocked the privy down
before the teacher could get out.

ALDEN NOWLAN

V. THE PURSE-PROUD PRELATE

WE LIVE IN A RICKETY HOUSE

We live in a rickety house,
  In a dirty dismal street,
Where the naked hide from day,
  And thieves and drunkards meet.

And pious folks with their tracts,
  When our dens they enter in,
They point to our shirtless backs,
  As the fruits of beer and gin.

And they quote us texts to prove
  That our hearts are hard as stone,
And they feed us with the fact
  That the fault is all our own.

It will be long ere the poor
  Will learn their grog to shun
While it's raiment, food and fire,
  And religion all in one.

I wonder some pious folks
  Can look us straight in the face,
For our ignorance and crime
  Are the Church's shame and disgrace.

We live in a rickety house,
  In a dirty dismal street,
Where the naked hide from day,
  And thieves and drunkards meet.

ALEXANDER McLACHLAN

PRECEPT AND EXAMPLE

Renounce the world, old Cassock cries,
  With vice and folly it abounds;
But yet, in worldly vanities,
  Cassock spends Twenty Thousand Pounds.

JOSEPH HOWE

REV. DR. BELLYGOD

Venter et praeterea nihil

Sworn scholiast of the bestial parts.
ROSSETTI

The Rev. Dr. Bellygod
  For dollars shows to heaven the way;
He treads the ways his fathers trod,
  As narrow-minded as were they.

A shiny hat and broadcloth sleek
  He always wears; his lengthy hair
With best Macassar oil doth reek,
  He has a very pious air.

He's never found among the poor,
  He's only anxious for rich sinners,
He's an experienced epicure,
  A chronic hunter of good dinners.

He is a staunch defender of
  The Church, the Bible and—Apicius;
The doctrine which he most doth love
  Is that one of the loaves and fishes.

Oft from the rostrum he is heard
  Of strong drink to condemn the use,
But from his beak 't may be inferred
  He freely quaffs the generous juice.

He heaves no end of amorous sighs,
  Of ladies' company he's fond;
For benedicts it would be wise
  To watch their wives when he's around.

'Tis whispered that he once was caught
In a surprising situation;
And that his influence was bought
For a rather doubtful speculation.

In the exploded right divine
Of kings he still believes; the masses
In ignorance he would have pine,
The football of the privileged classes.

He is particularly hard
On all who differ from him, he
Gloats over each poor wretch ill-starred,
His God's spite damns eternally.

He, pulpit-sheltered, bellows out
The hollow lies of creeds outworn;
But fearing he be put to rout
For argument he doesn't yearn.

A snob, he toadies to the high,
A blatant bigot, too, he is;
His little mind is darkened by
The unwholesome mists of prejudice.

Oh, not for you Doc Bellygod!
The mighty march of freedom stays.
So tread the ways your fathers trod,
And close your eyes to reason's rays.

JUDSON FRANCE

AN ARISTOCRATIC TRIO

'Mongst illustrious men in the Bible there be
King Domcome, Lord Howlong, and Baron Fig-tree.

JUDSON FRANCE

TWO THOUSAND YEARS OF PREACHING

The bearded figure sways like a tree in the blowing sand,
Haggard and lean-shanked as a prisoner-of-war;
Cries, "Repent ye for the Kingdom of Heaven is at hand!"
Draws up, like the sea in a cave, a deep murmur of awe.

Stock-still the circle stands, sick with nameless fear,
Like children at the sight of death round a broken bird.
Then suddenly it breaks like a bubble, scatters everywhere,
Like the scarecrows of Dogpatch or the Gadarene herd.

. . . .

The robed paunch bounces softly from the girdling zone
Of the polished pulpit, like a small well-found ship
Nuzzling her pier; and a rich, level tone
Calls for a change of values, with pursed lips.

And the nicely-dressed, day-dreaming congregation
Sits politely, simulating close attention;
With husband and wife in neat alternation,
And children doing things I will not mention.

GEOFFREY VIVIEN

BREBEUF AND HIS BRETHREN

When Lalemant and de Brébeuf, brave souls,
Were dying by the slow and dreadful coals
Their brother Jesuits in France and Spain
Were burning heretics with equal pain.
For both the human torture made a feast:
Then is priest savage, or Red Indian priest?

F. R. SCOTT

TO AN ULTRA PROTESTANT

Why rage and fret thee; only let them be:
The monkish rod, the sacerdotal pall,
Council and convent, Pope and Cardinal,
The black priest and his holy wizardry.
Nay, dread them not, for thought and liberty
Spread ever faster than the foe can smite,
And these shall vanish as the starless night
Before a morning mightier than the sea.
But what of thee and thine? That battle cry?
Those forms and dogmas that thou rear'st so high?
Those blasts of doctrine and those vials of wrath?
Thy hell for most and heaven for the few?
That narrow, joyless and ungenerous path?
What then of these? Ah, they shall vanish too!

ARCHIBALD LAMPMAN

IF I WERE THE DEVIL

If I were the Devil
down in Montreal
and had to get around
to do my dirty work
with the least possible fuss,

I'd simply rent space
beneath the flowing skirts
of these young priests walking
all over town:

and wouldn't have a worry,
I'd make out really fine.

RAYMOND SOUSTER

THE SCEPTIC

My Father Christmas passed away
When I was barely seven.
At twenty-one, alack-a-day,
I lost my hope of heaven.

Yet not in either lies the curse:
The hell of it's because
I don't know which loss hurt the worse—
My God or Santa Claus.

ROBERT W. SERVICE

DEACON ARNOLD

The "I love Jesus-ers"
 Are squawking at the church:
Deacon Arnold's leading them
 From a high perch.

Deacon Arnold keeps a store:
 Sugar, dry-goods, nails.
You should see him weighing coffee
 On his crooked scales.

Deacon Arnold never drinks,
 Never smokes nor swears:
And every time he shortens weight
 He lengthens out his prayers.

Deacon Arnold's love for Jesus
 So engrossed his life
That he couldn't love his neighbour
 Or his gentle wife;

Hadn't time to love the stars
 Or the drifting moon,

Or the white rain of the sun,
Dancing at high noon;

Or the singing green of water
Down an aisle of stone,
Or the wind on banks of roses
Making lovely moan.

Deacon Arnold sits to-night
On a lordly perch.
While all the "I love Jesus-ers"
Are squawking at the church.

WILSON MacDONALD.

THE IMMIGRANT

"Too many churches, not enough bawdy houses,"
the young Englishman fresh from the London flesh-pots
wrote to a friend after spending
his first week in Toronto (1885).

But later that year
was seduced in his own room by the daughter of an
Anglican minister,
and the next spring opened up the first
all-night mission on Yonge Street.

RAYMOND SOUSTER

JESUS SAVES

On my way to school
I used to pass
A Baptist church
And fields of grass.

"Jesus Saves"
Above the gate
Would comfort me
If I were late.

The church is gone,
The street is paved,
The Home Bank thrives
Where Jesus Saved.

IRVING LAYTON

INSURANCE
for Ron Everson

On the very dome
of their Holy of Holies
they've slung a lightning rod

just in case the good Lord
should someday slip up
the Mother Church won't
be left holding the bag.

RAYMOND SOUSTER

RESURRECTION OF ARP

On the third day rose Arp
out of the black sleeve of the tomb;
he could see like a cat in the dark
but the light left him dumb.

He stood up to testify,
and his tongue wouldn't work
in the old groove; he had to try
other tongues (including the Scandinavian).

The saints were all well pleased;
his periods rattled and rolled;
heresies scattered like ninepins;
all the tickets were sold.

When they turned down the gas
everybody could see there was
a halo of tongues of pale fire
licking the grease off his hair,

and a white bird
fluttered away in the rafters;
people heard
the breaking of a mysterious wind (laughter).

He spoke another language
majestic beautiful wild
holy superlative believable
and undefiled

by any comprehensible
syllable
to provoke dissent
or found a schism. . . .

After the gratifyingly large
number of converts had been given receipts
the meeting adjourned to the social hall
for sexual intercourse (dancing) and eats.

Arp talked to the reporters:
on the whole, was glad to have cheated the tomb,
though the angels had been "extremely courteous",
and death, after all, was only "another room".

A. J. M. SMITH

CAROL FOR THE INTERIM

Angels from the realms of glory
Sweetly singing o'er the plains,
Why does your familiar story
Most affect me when it rains?

Why does Christmas always find me
Wrapped in melancholy thought;
Private darkness always blind me
To the glory I have sought?

Teach me holier emotions
As your trumpets thrill the air:
Do you really want devotions
Dedicated in despair?

Brighten thou this sombre matin,
Christ descend, and speak to me;
Angels always sing in Latin
Tidings that are Greek to me.

Demonstrate how Bethlehem is
Solace for my special hell;
Grant me glory in extremis,
Consecrate my first Noel.

MICHAEL HORNYANSKY

VI. INDIGENOUS THROSTLES

THE CANADIAN AUTHORS MEET

Expansive puppets percolate self-unction
Beneath a portrait of the Prince of Wales.
Miss Crotchet's muse has somehow failed to function,
Yet she's a poetess. Beaming, she sails

From group to chattering group, with such a dear
Victorian saintliness, as is her fashion,
Greeting the other unknowns with a cheer—
Virgins of sixty who still write of passion.

The air is heavy with "Canadian" topics,
And Carman, Lampman, Roberts, Campbell, Scott,
Are measured for their faith and philanthropics,
Their zeal for God and King, their earnest thought.

The cakes are sweet, but sweeter is the feeling
That one is mixing with the *literati*;
It warms the old and melts the most congealing.
Really, it is a most delightful party.

Shall we go round the mulberry bush, or shall
We gather at the river, or shall we
Appoint a poet laureate this Fall,
Or shall we have another cup of tea?

O Canada, O Canada, Oh can
A day go by without new authors springing
To paint the native maple, and to plan
More ways to set the selfsame welkin ringing?

F. R. SCOTT

TO THE CANADIAN POETS

Come, my little eunuchs, my little virgins,
It is time you were home and in bed;
The wind is strong and cold on the streets
And it is almost eleven o'clock.

Soon the whores will be obvious at the corners
And I would not want you accosted or given the eye;
Soon the drunks will be turned out of the beverage rooms
And I would not have you raped in a dark lane.

Go, find your house and insert the key and put down the
night-lock.
Undress with the blinds down and touch the pillows, and
dream
Of Pickthall walking hand in hand with her fairies
And Lampman turning his back on Ottawa.

RAYMOND SOUSTER

CAN. LIT.

Since we had always sky about,
when we had eagles they flew out
leaving no shadow bigger than wren's
to trouble our most æromantic hens.
Too busy bridging loneliness to be alone
we hacked in ties what Emily etched in bone.
We French, we English, never lost our civil war,
endure it still, a bloodless civil bore;
no wounded lying about, no Whitman wanted.
It's only by our lack of ghosts we're haunted.

EARLE BIRNEY

AND SPOIL THE CHILD

(1931)

O Canada, our home, our native land!
Beset with breathy bards on every hand
We see thee rise, the true North, free and strong.
But where the strength, or freedom, in thy song?
Ah, Pope, thou shouldst be living at this time:
Learned and lewd alike we scribble rhyme.
And shall I listen only? Shall I not
Give back as ponderous verse as e'er I got?
I too have learn'd, as every school-child learns,
To censor Shakespeare, and admonish Burns;
Have mark'd where Milton's fire, and Dryden's, paled,
Where Chaucer falter'd, and where Shelley failed.

Train'd thus in blasting giants, shall I then
Restrain my thunderbolts from fellow-men?
When six of every seven that one sees
Are drooling verse with self-applausive ease,
Such stuff as dribbles down the nerveless gum
Swimming the uppermost saliva-scum:
Not mine, alas, Parnassus' peak to scale;
But seeing Poesy's poor patient tail
Bedevill'd with so many a tweak and twist
'Tis difficult to be no satirist.

See first where gentle Gallus gushes forth
Hymning the happy springtime of the North,
The sparkling drifts, or else the flaming trees,
In twenty thousand lines as like as peas.
How languidly the liquid lyrics loll
And dangle off into a dying fall,
As smooth as celluloid, or pulp-wood silk,
As toothsome and sustaining as skim milk.
While Swinburne, tumbling with unquiet breast,
Mutters, "I'm dead; for God's sake let me rest!"

Next, with a roll of never-muffled drums
The rattling chariot of Furius comes.
A Modern he, who brays a strident song
Like hoardings, vivid, and like garlic, strong;
Makes up in sputtering what he lacks in sense,
And to the nostril's, adds the ear's offence.

In panegyric next Pomposus struts.
Fair Canada's his theme, from soup to nuts.
No alley-cat so well his back-yard knows
As we the Northern Lights, th' eternal snows,
The sombre forests, and the mountains grand,
The flashing streams, the golden farming-land;
And still unask'd, unwearied bards rehearse
Unglorified topography in verse.

The open road, the tourist's out-of-doors
Bewitch battalions of ebullient bores,
While Inspiration huddles in his shell
And Truth still sulks, deep in her icy well.
O Canada, most patient of abstractions!—
These pallid piles of verbal petrifactions
Hide you from e'en your lovers' keenest sense.
Bring all your blizzards, quick, and blow them hence!

"But, but . . . " you say, "But, but . . . " But me no buts.
The one thing that our poets need is—guts.
One-half their work is bilge; the rest is rot:
The limp expression of a flabby thought.
And yet one trick might teach some few t'excel:
Write half as much, and write it twice as well.
Write what you must; and if another's said it,
Withdraw: you might as well; he'll get the credit.
More sternly think, then write, and if in doubt,
Rewrite, rewrite again, then chuck it out.

Are there none righteous then? Yes, X and Y
And sometimes Z, still wear their laurels high.

For these are flesh and blood, not skin and straw.
Is there one inch of all their skin flick'd raw
By the rude lash of this long-suffering tongue?
The gall'd jades wince; their withers are unwrung.
If others could, why don't they do the same?
The Critic, Sir, the Critic is to blame
Who with insulting clemency misuses
One rule for home, and one for foreign, muses.
Who'd face the labour of not being dull
When dullness is accounted wonderful?
Or who can value e'en deserved praise
When Harry, Dick, and Tom wear equal bays? . . .

* * *

See next, Lycoris brings a damp bouquet
Of pale emotions, bunch'd in neat array,
And misty meditations, maundering thin
"Through sense and nonsense, never out nor in."
A mild dejection mates with milder rage,
And passion simpers on each pallid page;
While stern reflection hews from out the breast
What oft was thought, but ne'er so ill exprest.

But tremble, critic! See Robustus stand
A swinging ballad clutch'd in either hand.
This sturdy weapon of an elder time
Will rip Detraction's ribs with rugged rhyme.
Yet tremble not: the jingling chain of sound
Most of its length, still drags along the ground.
The story sprawls and scrambles; when 'tis done
Fifty flat words usurp the place of one.

Humour! Dread Goddess! Most unpitying Muse!
Thee Bufo braves, and in no angel's shoes.
Seriously, well-meaningly designs
Uneasy arabesques of vapid lines,
Mocking the bellowings of thy boisterous cheeks,
Poor prattler, with such vague, pathetic squeaks—
Be gentle, Humour; merely at him laugh

And puff him from thee like a wisp of chaff,
Till in an inky ocean he shall drop
So small, so far, we shall not hear the plop.
Yet most the bards the tender lesson teach,
And puff the swelling brain-pan, each for each.
We arch the back, and stroke and purr by turns,
While "Hail, young Byron!" straight your "Wordsworth!"
earns.

. . . Perchance some day a traveller will pass
Where, stumbling idly through the weedy grass
A little dingy fallen stone he'll see,
And read, "Here lies Canadian Poetry:
Died, in a Hospital for Paralytics,
Smother'd in kindness by complacent critics."

L. A. MacKAY

ON READING AN ANTHOLOGY OF POPULAR POETRY

What shall we say now
To these whose shrill voice,
Giving the game away, now
Less by chance than by choice,

Cries from the stitched heart
In soft melodious screams
The sweet sweet songs that start
Out of alluvial dreams?

The old eternal frog
In the throat that comes
With the words *Mother, sweetheart, dog*
Excites, and then numbs.

Is there no katharsis
But "song" for this dull
Pain, that every Saul of Tarsus
Must pant himself into a Paul?

A. J. M. SMITH

EPIGRAMME

The produce of your pen
Is stiff with cellophane
That glitters while we strain
But will not let us in.

Your rhetoric sits tight
Within its self-made bars,
Your numbers are a night
Bereft of moon and stars.

If you intend to hide
The beauties of your mind,
Why leave one way untried?
Silence is so refined.

ROBERT FINCH

THE McGILL DAILY

"Why is *The McGill Daily*?"
Asked the pessimist sourly.
"Thank God," said the optimist gaily,
"That it isn't hourly!"

A. J. M. SMITH

THE TASTE OF SPACE

McLuhan put his telescope to his ear.
What a lovely smell, he said, we have here.

A. J. M. SMITH

THE LAYMAN TURNED CRITIC

Seeing an elephant, he cried with bliss:
"What a wonderful nightingale this is!"

And of a mosquito he observed with a laugh:
"What a curious thing is this giraffe."

LOUIS DUDEK

CONCOURSE AT CATARAQUI

There were of course those whom ease
        or a default of imagination
had made optimistic:
the backbone of the country
but slightly bent with perplexity.

There was the Muse's stepchild,
        an amuser:
a price on his English beard,
on his viewable grimace.

Also the hack fabulist
with no gift of words
for us: gain
            his criterion.

And one, a one-lunged
trumpeter
            who denied
long, long before cockcrow
—hollow-chested.

And Cowardice hiding out
    behind a circus show of reason:
hardest he was to smoke out.

IRVING LAYTON

THE DEATH OF THE POETESS

Her collected works
Published at last
Alas just before.
Here are the 32
Little white grave-stones
Engraved on both sides
With epitaphs.

She was a spire that dreams
In a rocking-chair
Or a spire laid sideways
On a sofa.
A spire that sipped tea,
A soft pink spire.
In her illness
Books fell from her bed
Like heavy marble leaves
(As they fall in Vallombrosa)
From a marble tree.
Now the clock that is her heart
Tick-tocks itself to stop.
Beside her corpse
Lies the Collected Edition
32
Thin gravestones.

JAMES REANEY

MISUNDERSTANDING

I placed
my hand
upon
her thigh.

By the way
she moved
away
I could see
her devotion
to literature
was not
perfect.

IRVING LAYTON

ON READING CERTAIN POEMS & EPISTLES BY IRVING LAYTON & LOUIS DUDEK

Hail Coprophilia, muse of Layton, hail!
Doxy of Dudek, skoal! who drop'st in pail
Thick steaming words and brownish lumps of rhyme—
Manure essential in this barren clime,
Where Saxon critics without guts or gall
Praise these thy sons but little, if at all.
Yet these are they who vindicate thy cause,
Who preach thy gospel and affirm thy laws:
Blest pair of poets, put on earth by thee
To sweat and strain and groan to set us free
From Anglo-philistine hypocrisy.
What shovelfuls of praise we ought to pay
These swart forerunners of an Augean day
Let us with candour, clangour, and no taste,
Make haste to proffer, oh make haste, make haste!
Layton shall how to flatter Layton teach,
And modest Dudek Dudek's glories preach;
Layton shall tingle in Canadian air,
And echo answer *Dudek* everywhere;
In ev'ry quarterly and magazine
Their linkèd names in squibs and puffs be seen;
Letters to editors be filled with them,
And gratitude replace each critic's phlegm:
Repentant Wilson, Smith, MacLure, and Frye
Shall who can praise them loudest longest, try.

A. J. M. SMITH

TO IRVING LAYTON, ON HIS LOVE POEM TO MRS. JACQUELINE KENNEDY, THEN FIRST LADY

Come off it, cocky Layton, what has Jackie got
Save place and face and fortune sweet Aviva's not?
But if you want variety to warm old bones,
Stick to the Commonwealth: try Mrs. Armstrong-Jones.

A. J. M. SMITH

LINES

Addressed to a dozen young Canadian Poets, after unwisely Devouring five Little Magazines at a Sitting

Enough, enough.   Gentlemen, I protest

Over and over and over
These mementoes of your fornications
Vignettes of your sensitive childhood
Kicks from jazz,
And all these poetics about poetics about poetics
And the fearsome insults and the fulsome accolades
AND your girl-friend's vulva
AND your trip to Mexico

Please, gentlemen, please.

JOHN GLASSCO

A CURSE ON THOSE WHO KISS AND TELL

A curse on those who kiss and tell
But keep the hottest spot in hell
For those who go from bad to worse
In other words from bed to verse.

JOE WALLACE

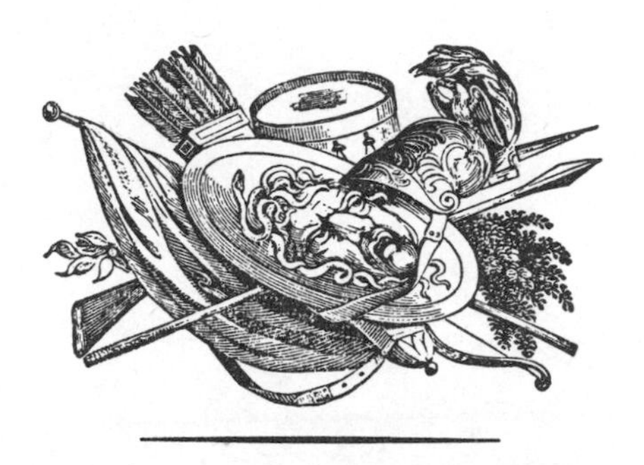

VII. WE STAND ON GUARD

WAR ON THE PERIPHERY

Around the battlements go by
Soldier men, against the sky—
Violent lovers, husbands, sons,
Guarding my peaceful life with guns.

My pleasures, how discreet they are:
A little booze, a little car,
Two little children and a wife
Living a small suburban life.

My little children eat my heart;
At seven o'clock we kiss and part,
At seven o'clock we meet again;
They eat my heart and grow to men.

I watch their tenderness with fear
While on the battlements I hear
The violent, obedient ones,
Guarding my family with guns.

GEORGE JOHNSTON

THE ANNEXATION OF NATAL

August 8, 1843

When we in touch with heathens come,
We send them first a case of rum,
Next, to rebuke their native sin,
We send a missionary in:
Then when the hungry Hottentot
Has boiled his pastor in a pot,
We teach him Christian, dumb contrition,
By means of dum-dum ammunition,
  The situation grows perplexed,
  The wicked country is annexed:
But, Oh! the change when o'er the wild,
Our sweet Humanity has smiled:
The savage shaves his shaggy locks,
Wears breeches and balbriggan socks,
Learns Euclid, classifies the fossils,
Draws pictures of the Twelve Apostles—
And now his pastor at the most,
He is content to simply roast:
  Forgetful of the art of war,
  He smokes a twenty-cent cigar,
  He drinks not rum, his present care is
  For whisky and Apollinaris.
Content for this his land to change,
He fattens up and dies of mange.
  Lo! on the ashes of his Kraal,
  A Protestant Ca-the-der-al!

STEPHEN LEACOCK

ANGLO-JAPANESE ALLIANCE

August 12, 1905

Valiant, noble Japanee,
Listen to Britannia's plea,

Since the battle of Yalu,
I've been yearning all for you;
Since the fight at Meter Hill
Other suitors make me ill;
Tell me not of German beaux
Addle-headed, adipose,
Double-barrelled Dutchman plain,
Sullen, sombre sons of Spain,
Flaxen Swede, Roumanian red,
Fickle Frenchmen, underfed,
  Nay, I care for none of these
  Take me, O my Japanese,
Yamagata, you of Yeddo,
Fold me, hold me to your heart
Togo, take me to Tokio,
Tell me not that we must part;
  In your home at Nagasaki
  Cuddle me against your Khaki,
Since the Russians couldn't tan you,
Rule, I pray you, Rule Britannia!

STEPHEN LEACOCK

LEST WE FORGET

The British troops at the Dardanelles
Were blown to bits by British shells
  Sold to the Turks by Vickers.
And many a brave Canadian youth
Will shed his blood on foreign shores,
And die for Democracy, Freedom, Truth,
With his body full of Canadian ores,
Canadian nickel, lead, and scrap,
Sold to the German, sold to the Jap,
  With Capital watching the tickers.

F. R. SCOTT

BATTLE HYMN OF THE SPANISH REBELLION

The Church's one foundation
Is now the Moslem sword,
In meek collaboration
With flame, and axe, and cord;
While overhead are floating,
Deep-winged with holy love,
The battle planes of Wotan,
The bombing planes of Jove.

L. A. MacKAY

TWO SNARLS OF A DISGUSTED COLONIAL

I

Freedom in Spain, exhaled a groan.
Her champion, England, scribbling notes,
Refused as yet to throw a stone,
And only held the stoners' coats.

II

Let Britain's leaders, if they choose,
Be cushions for Benito's hips,
And lick the heels of Adolf's shoes.
But damn them! must they smack their lips?

L. A. MacKAY

POLITICAL INTELLIGENCE

Nobody said Apples for nearly a minute—
I thought I should die.*
Finally, though, the second sardine
from the end, on the left,
converted a try.
(It brought down the house.
The noise was terrific.
I dropped my glass eye.)

Meanwhile the P.M.
managed to make himself heard.
He looked sad
but with characteristic aplomb said
Keep calm there is no cause for alarm.

Two soldiers' crutches
crossed up a little bit of fluff
from a lint bandage
in the firing chamber of a 12-inch gun.
People agreed not to notice.
The band played a little bit louder.
It was all very British.

A. J. M. SMITH

KIRKLAND LAKE

1943

Under the dark industrial sky
we wonder why we have to die
who living, were valued at a wage
that starved our youth and murdered age.
Or why engage for tyrants here
to end the tyranny of fear,
whose quarrel is with all of those
the heavens of our desire that close?
For justice undertake a cause
that has no justice in its laws,
but claims for unity the right
forbids the citizen unite.
For thirty dollars shall we sell
our happiness to mend their hell,
to save their cuckoos, clear our nest,
redeem by our unrest their rest
and fight for freedom who are not free?
Let freemen die, but why should we
who toil to set the rich on high

three shifts beneath the smoking sky?
Let those who call on us to keep
their freedom safe and safe their sleep
account and pledge us higher for
the wealth and peace our griefs ensure:
a week-end fit for play like theirs
and futures guaranteed from cares,
evenings when not too tired a man
his leisures takes and pleasure can,
a chance for more than daily bread—
their daughters for our sons to wed,
so working and in wanting we
may equal them and be as free.
But till that day let them not cry
upon our loyal sons to die,
who with our usual logic see
they die for freedom that are free.

JAMES WREFORD

THE USE OF FORCE

Please don't believe
The use of force
Is how we change the social course;
The use of force
You surely know
Is how we keep the status quo.

JOHN K. ROOKE

IN THIS VERANDAH

In this verandah of the August heart
sanguine with awnings rest the grey old girls,
Clotho in a deck chair
        Behind the sandbags
        in the Victoria & Albert

sandalsocks for the Legion
A.D. 400
showing a knowledge of knit and purl
Now at the thread's end the mottled finger
weaves for the arching airboy.
Lachesis fumbles the skein, arthritic.
Beyond the awnings beyond
the shrinking waters the blind
beldame snips with the chromium shears
and you and I and the burnished amateurs
at Cawnpore and Singapore
Inkerman and Rotterdam
Mafeking and Chungking
and Marathon I and II
(and III?)
are ravelled in the wool.
No need here to beat open the mind
no fire exits from the Minotaur.
Make your hearts into cordite
nipple them with steel
and suffer this propulsion
knowing only that the sun outlasts,
the beautiful bright coyote
will outflank the awnings
outsit the three bitches.

EARLE BIRNEY

#70 ARMY RECEPTION CENTRE, FREDERICTON, N.B.

That year they scraped the barrel
for the very last time,
with us right at the bottom—

farm-boys in overalls
and laced-up knee-boots
a few city boys
with all the answers.

I remember reading Hemingway
in the smoky barracks
waiting the call
for the gaze up the rectum
the intelligence test
the over-friendly examiner;

and every evening
walked over the bridge
across their wide river
to where the bad girls
were supposed to live,

while the newly-arrived
veterans of the far-off war
sat around in the corridors
with their arms or legs missing
waiting for discharge:

(waiting being just
another name for the army).

RAYMOND SOUSTER

HERO'S REWARD

For this he quartered flaming skies
outwitting gremlins, dodging flak,
nor guessed the fate awaiting him,
his lousy lot if he came back—

to walk a dog a dirty night
and guard it from the muddy ditch
and lead it home again and see
it cuddled by a scolding bitch.

GEORGE WALTON

PSALM 23

Revised Version

The Christian's my keeper; I shall not want.
He letteth me to eat in rock pastures;
He slaketh me beside the salt waters.
He visas my soul;
He heedeth me with the stamp of righteousness for his
name's sake.
Yea, though I crawl through the alleys of the countries
of death,
I will fear no sanction: for thou art with me;
Committee and staff they comfort me.
Thou preparest a paper about me in the presence of mine
enemies:
Thou anointest mine ear with words; my cup runneth over.
Purely Aryan blood-cells may flow for all the days of
thy life,
But I will dwell in the blood of the Lord for ever.

RALPH GUSTAFSON

ON THE STRUMA MASSACRE

Now as these slaughtered seven hundreds hear
The vulgar sennet of thine angel sound,
Grant, in thy love, that they may see that ground
Whose promised acres holy footsteps bear.
For they of only this made credulous prayer—
Even for whom thy Son the tempest bound
And waters walked O not those same where, drowned,
Driven by plausible tongues and mute despair,
These faithful roll! No not as they, with board
And spike, who took Thy sweetness then, do we—
Studied in ignorance, and knowing Thee.
For Thine archaic crown of thorns and cord,
Statistics are become Thine agony,
The ocean designate, Gabbatha, Lord.

RALPH GUSTAFSON

From NEW WINGS FOR ICARUS

In the one-two domestic goose one-two one-two step
of our left-right modern one-two times one-two
we march left-right singing one-two
onward left-right christian soldiers
lift up your one-two hearts and legs
and rifles up up up cocked and down
with the foe we kill for chrissake one-two
hallelujah we're on the move again
left-right one-two New Jerusalem
is just left-right around the corner
we are all brothers big brothers
serving one-two time in battle dress
we must all stick together one-two
god-fearing left-right law-abiding
swelling together our ranks and numbers
swelling our pride swelling our purse
swelling breasts buttocks bellies
one-two one-two one-two swollen privates
pick 'em up, brother, up up up
pride of disney- and motherland up to his knees left-right
in bible blood and imperial oil
recruit one-nine-eight-four
defender of the new left-right
faith in international business
machines, brave for the new one-two
world of baptized walkie-talkies
left-right of course there is always
one-two the human one-two element
cream of emotion faith tranquillizer
hope salts charity pills love shots
don't hug that gun like a girl, man
one-two left-right one-two the girl
one-two who loves one-two
a soldier one-two is part one-two
of the grand cavalcade: it all adds up
to nineteenhundredandeightyfour

answers to a single question
what d'hell you think this is—
    a fuckin' funeral parade?
quick march left-right one-two one-two
threeandahalf die every two seconds
ten are born every three seconds
twohundred ejaculations per minute on target
to say nothing of the intercepted ones
over sixthousand burials per hour
ebb and tide of semen and sand
on the bluff shores of time
which way to turn for escape?
abooout face! one-two one-two
nineteenhundredandeightyfour
questions and a single answer
the old man's army is the best goddam
    fightin' machine there is, get it?
triumph of left-right law and one-two order
of the jungle of mathematics—regimental
orders regimental colours regimental
prayers in *nomine patriae*
one-two left-right *et ficti* . . .

HENRY BEISSEL

VIII. PRIVATE HELLS

OUTMODED WISDOM

(Or The Diversions of the Seven Sages)

I. PITTACUS

Endure, my soul, endure and be thou dumb,
Knowing, though this be ill, yet worse will come.

II. SOLON

Set me his statue up in alabaster
Who ends one single day without disaster.

III. THALES

Men mock the foolish wisdom of the wise;
Moles think men over-rate the worth of eyes.

IV. BIAS

Two wrongs won't make a right: the odds are long
That two rights, though, will make at least one wrong.

V. PERIANDER

Tell not your voters, "Thus you gain your ends,"
My statesman; tell them, "Thus you spite your friends."

VI. CLEOBULUS

To bring mine enemy down in black despair,
I prayed, "May the gods grant his every prayer."

VII. ANACHARSIS

Why, they're all cynics! What's a cynic, then?
—A man that can enjoy his fellow-men.

L. A. MacKAY

EURYNOME

Come all old maids that are squeamish
And afraid to make mistakes,
Don't clutter your lives up with boyfriends,
The nicest girls marry snakes.

If you don't mind slime on your pillow
And caresses as gliding as ice
—Cold skin, warm heart, remember,
And besides, they keep down the mice—

If you're really serious-minded,
It's the best advice you can take:
No rumpling, no sweating, no nonsense,
Oh who would not sleep with a snake?

JAY MACPHERSON

HAIL WEDDED LOVE

Oh the many joys of a harlot's wedding,
Countless as the ticks that tumble in the bedding!
All knives are out and slicing fast,
The bread-oven goes with a furnace-blast,
Drink flows like sea-water, cock crows till dawn,
The children of Bedlam riot in the corn.

The nymphs of Bridewell leave their fountains
To come and dance on the blockish mountains,
The meadow shoots cuckoo-pint all over
And Venus-flytrap common as clover,
The goat-shagged fiddler with urgent bow
Drives on the measure of boot and toe,
The bridegroom woos, "My bird, my cunny,
My jam, my pussy, my little pot of honey—"

Well, delight attend their pillow!
And I'll go seek a bending willow!
To hang my silent harp upon
Beside the river of Babylon.

JAY MACPHERSON

SOUR WINE

I met the wife who'd left me bed,
  The wife I'd loved so true,
Wid a faded shawl on her ould head
  And a scowl that'd stab ye through.

She eased her barrow of turf and stood
  Wide-beamed in her rain-soaked clogs—
Yet wanst we'd kissed as lovers could,
  And then fought like cats and dogs!

"You're lookin' your worst, you mangy cur,"
  Says she, the damned ould cat.
"May you blister in hell," I answered her
  And let it go at that.

ARTHUR STRINGER

I WISH MY TONGUE

I wish my tongue were a quiver the size of a huge cask,
Packed and crammed with long black venomous rankling darts.
I'd fling you more full of them, and joy in the task,
Than ever Sebastian was, or Caesar, with thirty-three swords
  in his heart.

I'd make a porcupine out of you, or a pincushion, say;
The shafts should stand so thick you'd look like a headless hen
Hung up by the heels, with the long bare red neck stretching,
  curving, and dripping away
From the soiled floppy ball of ruffled feathers standing on end.

You should bristle like those cylindrical brushes they use to
  scrub out bottles,
Not even to reach the kindly earth with the soles of your
  prickled feet;
And I should stand by and watch you wriggle and writhe,
  gurgling through the barbs in your throttle,
Like a woolly caterpillar pinned on its back—man, that would
  be sweet!

L. A. MacKAY

A PORTRAIT, AND A PROPHECY

Indeed, he has sinned! and of his many sins the chief
That mortal sin, Himself. A delicate-fingered thief
Of values this, a dealer in stolen belief,

And a smiling falsifier of the intricate debt
Of love to the tiger. Why! this is the one who set
A premium on the monstrous sins of age and let

The petty faults of youth go hang, who watered his blood
And coached his infected heart to stammer *I will be good*
Like a young Victoria of wax and wood—

And now, by God! he has fallen in love with Penitence!
He'll bring that slut to bed of the most fulsome of his sins,
The precocious blue-eyed bastard, Innocence.

* * *

Cassandra-like, I prophesy the lad
So sired will grow from not-so-good to bad:
Untruthful, nasty, secretive, and sad,
He'll drive his ill-adjusted mother mad,
And end by growing up just like his dad.

A. J. M. SMITH

FREAK SHOW

Perhaps some day the Professor's fleas may pull
In gilded coach The Thinnest Man in The World
Together with his bride The Crocodile Girl
Up to the doors of the church where The Armless
    Woman
Waits to throw confetti with her skilful toes;

And together with the best man The Tattooed Giant
And the bridesmaid the demure Leopard Girl,

They will walk altarwards with the music of The
Bearded Brothers
Loud in their ears, where The King Of The Midgets,
Modest J.P., will perform the nuptials;

With The Half Man puffing calmly at his cigar
In the front row, and the impatient clamour
Of flea-hoofs sounding outside upon the cobbles.

RAYMOND SOUSTER

THE IMPROVED BINOCULARS

Below me the city was in flames:
the fireman were the first to save
themselves. I saw steeples fall on their knees.

I saw an agent kick the charred bodies
from an orphanage to one side, marking
the site carefully for a future speculation.

Lovers stopped short of the final spasm
and went off angrily in opposite directions,
their elbows held by giant escorts of fire.

Then the dignitaries rode across the bridges
under an arcade of light which delighted them,
noting for later punishment those that went before.

And the rest of the populace, their mouths
distorted by an unusual gladness, bawled thanks
to this comely and ravaging ally, asking

Only for more light with which to see
their neighbour's destruction.

All this I saw through my improved binoculars.

IRVING LAYTON

CHRIST WALKS IN THIS INFERNAL DISTRICT TOO

Beneath the Malebolge lies Hastings Street,
The province of the pimp upon his beat,
Where each in his little world of drugs or crime
Moves helplessly or, hopeful, begs a dime
Wherewith to purchase half a pint of piss—
Although he will be cheated, even in this.
I hope, although I doubt it, God knows
This place where chancres blossom like the rose,
For on each face is such a hard despair
That nothing like a grief could enter there.
And on this scene from all excuse exempt
The mountains gaze in absolute contempt,
Yet this is also Canada, my friend,
Yours to absolve of ruin, or make an end.

MALCOLM LOWRY

THE CITY OF THE END OF THINGS

Beside the pounding cataracts
Of midnight streams unknown to us
'Tis builded in the leafless tracts
And valleys huge of Tartarus.
Lurid and lofty and vast it seems;
It hath no rounded name that rings,
But I have heard it called in dreams
The City of the End of Things.

Its roofs and iron towers have grown
None knoweth how high within the night,
But in its murky streets far down
A flaming terrible and bright
Shakes all the stalking shadows there,
Across the walls, across the floors,
And shifts upon the upper air

From out a thousand furnace doors;
And all the while an awful sound
Keeps roaring on continually,
And crashes in the ceaseless round
Of a gigantic harmony.
Through its grim depths re-echoing
And all its weary height of walls,
With measured roar and iron ring,
The inhuman music lifts and falls.
Where no thing rests and no man is,
And only fire and night hold sway;
The beat, the thunder and the hiss
Cease not, and change not, night nor day.
And moving at unheard commands,
The abysses and vast fires between,
Flit figures that with clanking hands
Obey a hideous routine;
They are not flesh, they are not bone,
They see not with the human eye,
And from their iron lips is blown
A dreadful and monotonous cry;
And whoso of our mortal race
Should find that city unaware,
Lean Death would smite him face to face,
And blanch him with its venomed air:
Or caught by the terrific spell,
Each thread of memory snapt and cut,
His soul would shrivel and its shell
Go rattling like an empty nut.

It was not always so, but once,
In days that no man thinks upon,
Fair voices echoed from its stones,
The light above it leaped and shone:
Once there were multitudes of men,
That built that city in their pride,
Until its might was made, and then
They withered age by age and died.

But now of that prodigious race,
Three only in an iron tower,
Set like carved idols face to face,
Remain the masters of its power;
And at the city gate a fourth,
Gigantic and with dreadful eyes,
Sits looking toward the lightless north,
Beyond the reach of memories;

Fast rooted to the lurid floor,
A bulk that never moves a jot,
In his pale body dwells no more,
Or mind or soul,—an idiot!
But some time in the end those three
Shall perish and their hands be still,
And with the master's touch shall flee
Their incommunicable skill.
A stillness absolute as death
Along the slacking wheels shall lie,
And, flagging at a single breath,
The fires shall moulder out and die.
The roar shall vanish at its height,
And over that tremendous town
The silence of eternal night
Shall gather close and settle down.
All its grim grandeur, tower and hall,
Shall be abandoned utterly,
And into rust and dust shall fall
From century to century;
Nor ever living thing shall grow,
Nor trunk of tree, nor blade of grass;
No drop shall fall, no wind shall blow,
Nor sound of any foot shall pass;
Alone of its accursed state,
One thing the hand of Time shall spare,
For the grim Idiot at the gate
Is deathless and eternal there.

ARCHIBALD LAMPMAN

NOTES

3 CANADA: CASE HISTORY. From *The Strait of Anian*, Toronto, 1948.

3 FROM COLONY TO NATION. From *Music on a Kazoo*, Toronto, 1956.

4 COLD COLLOQUY. From "Poem on Canada", in *The White Centre*, Toronto, 1945.

7 FOUND OBJECT. From *Abracadabra*, Toronto, 1967.

8 NATIONAL IDENTITY. From *Maclean's* Magazine, June, 1963.

11 SONG. From *The Emigrant and Other Poems*, Toronto, 1861. Alexander McLachlan (1818-96), was a tailor's apprentice in Glasgow who emigrated to Canada in 1840. He established himself on a clearing near Guelph. His early poems are filled with a nostalgic love of the motherland, but by 1863 he had returned to Britain on a lecture tour to encourage emigration.

12 YOUNG CANADA. From the same volume. This crude but spirited attack on the Canadian politician reminds us of John A. Macdonald's bitter remark that the job of the politician was to climb the tree "and shake down the acorns to the pigs below".

14 PLACES. Joseph Howe, the Nova Scotian political leader and journalist. From his commonplace-book. Quoted in Chester Martin, *Empire and Commonwealth*, Oxford, 1929, p. 159.

14 THE MEMBER OF PARLIAMENT. From *Comber Cove*, Toronto, 1937.

15 BATTLE OF YONGE STREET, 1837. From *Rhymes*, London, Ontario, 1871. The fiasco described in this rough parody of Campbell's *Hohenlinden* was the "military" turning-point of the rebellion in Upper Canada, when, to quote A. R. M. Lower (*Colony to Nation*, p. 242) "both sides behaved in the best traditions of comic opera".

16 A WORD TO THE FINNIGANS. From the same. The "Finnigans" are the Fenians, an Irish nationalist society whose raids into Canada in the 1860's helped solidify pro-Confederation feeling in Canada.

17 DAMN YANKEES, 1830. From the same. Modern title supplied by the editors. These stanzas occur in a long poem describing Glendinning's voyage from Scotland and the trip via New York, the Hudson River, Albany, and the Mohawk Valley to Lake Ontario and finally to Scarborough. Glendinning apparently came to Canada in the 1830's. The poem contains one vivid stanza that ought to be preserved here:

Ye thinkna of poor luckless wretches
In a ship's hold and under hatches
'Mang twa three hunder lowsie bitches
Brood of blue ruin!
These, as the vessel rolls and pitches,
Cursin' and spuein'.

18 LE TOMBEAU DE PIERRE FALCON. From *Poetry 62*. This poem is a free translation of one in French by the Métis poet Pierre Falcon. The original is to be found in Hargreave's *Red River*, Montreal, 1871.

20 TO TENNYSON. The volume from which this poem is taken is rare. The full title of the book is *Muse Whangs*, and the subtitle is "Poems Amorous, Bacchanalian, Political, Memorial, Humorous, and Miscellaneous". After the author's name is appended the phrase "Citizen of Toronto". The publisher is given as follows: Printed at the Sign of the Will-o'-the-Wisp, 1887. The author was clearly a classical scholar, an anti-clerical socialist, influenced by Anacreon, Byron and Swinburne. Tennyson was elevated to the peerage in 1884. The second of these two poems was the result of the author's annoyance at Tennyson's political gradualism as expressed in the much admired lines *You ask me why, tho' ill at ease.*

23 THE PRINCE'S VISIT, 1860. The Prince was Edward, later Edward VII, who arrived in Montreal in 1860 for the opening of the Victoria Bridge, and later continued his tour through the States. De Cordova is an American, as the text makes clear. Some Canadian poets, including Sangster and McLachlan, wrote eulogies on this occasion.

25 THE ROYAL VISIT. From *The Red Heart*, Toronto, 1949. This visit was during the Dominion tour of George VI and Queen Elizabeth in 1939.

25 FRANKIE WENT DOWN TO THE CORNER. First published in the *Canadian Forum*, later in *The Ill-Tempered Lover*, 1948. The puritanical liquor laws of Ontario have been somewhat ameliorated since the poem was written, though it still is not without some relevance.

27 AUDACITY. From *Signature*, Vancouver, 1964.

29 BALLADE OF MEDDLERS. From *Complete Poems of Tom MacInnes*, Toronto, 1923.

30 THE MONARCH OF THE ID. From *Trial of a City*, Toronto, 1952.

32 LETTER TO A LIBRARIAN. From *A Laughter in the Mind*, Toronto, 1958. The book of poems "torn up" was *The Blue Propeller*, 1955.

32 A LASS IN WONDERLAND. From *Signature*, Vancouver, 1964.

34 DIALECTICS. First published in *Preview*, Jan., 1943; in *The Colour as Naked*, Toronto, 1953.

35 THE MODERN POLITICIAN. From *The Poems of Archibald Lampman*, edited with a Memoir by Duncan Campbell Scott, Toronto, 1900.

35 TO A RESTLESS POLITICIAN. From *The Wayward Queen*, Toronto, n.d.

36 W.L.M.K. From *The Eye of the Needle*, Montreal, 1957.

37 ELECTION DAY. Written in Victoria, B.C.; from *As Ten As Twenty*, Toronto, 1946.

39 PARLIAMENTARY LIBRARY: OTTAWA. From *Place of Meeting*, Toronto, 1960.

39 BUSINESS AS USUAL. From *Flowers for Hitler*, Toronto, 1964.

40 POLITICAL MEETING. From *The Rocking Chair*, Toronto, 1948. Camillien Houde was the famous Mayor of Montreal who was in and out of office (out in a concentration camp 1941-5 for opposing National Registration) between 1930 and 1955. An ardent Quebec nationalist, he flirted with fascism and anti-semitism, yet his engaging personality and sense of humour made him something of a legend even among his political opponents.

41 M. BERTRAND. From *The Rocking Chair*, Toronto, 1948.

42 MONSIEUR GASTON. From *The Rocking Chair*, Toronto, 1948.

43 THE WAY THE WORLD ENDS. From *The Improved Binoculars*, Toronto, 1956.

44 BONNE ENTENTE. First published in *Saturday Night*, March, 1954; in *Events & Signals*, 1954.

44 THE STATUS OF CANADIAN GEOLOGY. From *The New Yorker*, December 14, 1957.

45 A CHURCH SEEN IN CANADA. From *An Acre in the Seed*, Cambridge, Mass., 1949. Theodore Spencer was former Boylston Professor of English at Harvard, poet and critic. This was written at North Hatley, Quebec, where he spent several summers and became enamoured of Quebec place names.

45 HOMO CANADENSIS. From *The Cariboo Horses*, Toronto, 1965.

47 A SOVEREIGN NATION. From *A Radiant Sphere*, Moscow, 1964.

47 AT THE TOURIST CENTER IN BOSTON. Uncollected.

49 THE ONLY TOURIST IN HAVANA. From *Flowers for Hitler*, Toronto, 1964.

53 THE WORKMAN'S SONG. From *The Emigrant and Other Poems*, Toronto, 1861. The first three stanzas of thirteen. The poem goes on to tell how McLachlan (or the workman) finds comfort in recalling his kinship with the breed of Knox, reading the bards (mainly, one assumes, Burns) and remembering the songs of the birds in the forests of the homeland. It is significant that both McLachlan and the Irishman Standish O'Grady entitled their most ambitious volumes *The Emigrant*, not *The Immigrant*.

53 ON OSTENTATION. From *The Mackenzie Poems*, Toronto, 1966.

54 TO A MILLIONAIRE. From *The Poems of Archibald Lampman*, edited with a Memoir by Duncan Campbell Scott, Toronto, 1900.

54 FIVE-PER-CENT. From *Bar Room Ballads*, 1940.

56 HYMN TO THE GLORY OF FREE ENTERPRISE. First published in *The Nation*, New York, 18 March, 1944. Set to music by the author, it was sung with great success in the Toronto Revue "Spring Thaw", 1954. The solos by the various Presidents are close paraphrases of remarks by certain prominent Canadians who visited Ottawa during World War II.

59 PANIC. From *A Radiant Sphere*, Moscow, 1964.

59 FOR THE RECORD. From *New Wave: Canada*, edited by Raymond Souster, Toronto, 1966.

60 THE SERVICE CLUB. From *Comber Cove*, Toronto, 1937.

62 A PSALM OF MONTREAL. First published in *The Spectator*, London, 1878; reprinted in *The Note-Books of Samuel Butler*, edited by H. Festing Jones.

63 THE FOOTBALL MATCH. From *Songs of the Great Dominion*, edited by W. D. Lighthall, 1897. This spirited piece is perhaps only mildly satiric but we could not resist including it for its engaging gusto. There was at least no taint of professionalism or American infiltration in the bloody brawl immortalized here.

65 THE CANADIAN SOCIAL REGISTER. First published in *Saturday Night*, March, 1949; in *Events & Signals*, 1954.

68 LISTED. From *The Strength of the Hills*, Toronto, 1948.

68 SATURDAY SUNDAE. First published in *Preview*, March, 1944; in *Overture*, Toronto, 1945.

69 THE PENGUIN. The author writes that this poem was probably published in the Toronto *Varsity* in 1948 or 1949 and appeared in the Merton College magazine *The Postmaster*, 1952-3. He is not, as was wrongly stated in our first edition, the only Canadian to win the Newdigate Prize at Oxford. Professor Frank Underhill has called our attention to the fact that E. W. McInnis, now a distinguished Canadian historian, also won

the Newdigate—much to the disgust of his competitor, the English historian A. L. Rowse, who remarks rather scornfully in his book *A Cornishman at Oxford* that the prize was carried off by an "unknown Canadian Rhodes scholar", while his own entry merely received a *proxime accessit*. "So much," he said, "for the judgment of the Oxford dons in the matter of art."

70 HOW BLACK WAS MY CADILLAC. From CIV/n, 1955.

72 GOLFERS. From *The Blue Propeller*, 1955.

72 THE LIFELESS WIFE. From *Poetry 64*, edited by John Robert Colombo, Toronto, 1964.

73 SINALÓA. From *Ice Cod Bell or Stone*, Toronto, 1962.

74 ANGLOSAXON STREET. From *Now Is Time*, Toronto, 1945. Toronto is evidently the locale of this skilful satire.

75 ANGLO-CANADIAN. From *Music on a Kazoo*, 1956.

75 ON THE APPOINTMENT, etc. First published in *The Blasted Pine*, 1957.

76 THE CALL OF THE WILD. From *The Eye of the Needle*, Montreal, 1957.

76 FESTIVAL AT STRATFORD. From *Sonata for Frog and Man*, Toronto, 1959.

77 LEDA IN STRATFORD, ONT. From *The Tamarack Review*, No. 41, Winter 1966.

77 ODE TO FREDERICTON. First published in *The Blasted Pine*, 1957.

78 FREDERICTON. From *Selected Poems*, Toronto, 1956.

78 LOCAL BOY. From the *Canadian Forum*, October, 1952.

79 SOUVENIRS DU TEMPS PERDU. First published in *Here & Now*, May, 1948; in *A Sort of Ecstasy*, 1954.

80 LANDLADY. From *As Ten As Twenty*, Toronto, 1946.

81 FUNERAL OF AN ADMINISTRATOR. From *Deeper into the Forest*, Toronto, 1948.

82 THE CONVICT HOLOCAUST. From the *Canadian Forum*, June, 1930; in *New Provinces*, Toronto, 1936.

82 THE HANGING. From *West by East*, Toronto, 1933. The author was one of the Group of Seven and Principal of the Ontario College of Art.

87 WINTER IN LOWER CANADA. From *The Emigrant*, Montreal, 1842. Not much is known about Standish O'Grady. He was born in Ireland, educated at Trinity College, Dublin, an impoverished clergyman, resolved on emigration to America as a last resort. Arrived at

Quebec in 1836 and took a small farm at Sorel on the south bank of the St. Lawrence. Suffered severely from the cold and disliked the French Canadians. Felt Upper Canada to be "a far more desirable emporium for our redundant population". The French Canadians shared this view. He planned *The Emigrant* as a poem in four cantos, but completed only one, though this consisted of more than a thousand heroic couplets, mostly pretty dull.

88 THE BACHELOR IN HIS SHANTY. From *Scottish Canadian Poets*, edited by Daniel Clark, Toronto, 1900. Boyd was brought to Canada at the age of three from Ayrshire; died in Guelph, Ontario, 1880. One of the many Scottish Canadian farmer poets influenced by Burns.

90 ANNANDALE FARMING. From *Rhymes*, London, Ontario, 1871. Three stanzas of five. The conditions described belong to the 1830's. Perhaps the most significant lines in the poem are "And we will be your servants as 'tis meet . . . And never speak a word on politics." Both Glendinning and Alexander McLachlan, though proletarian poets who brought the sentiments of Chartist discontent and of Burns' humanitarianism with them from the Old World, knew their places, and once their industry and thrift had won for them the battle of the wilderness, they became sturdy, conservative, patriotic versifiers.

91 From EPISTLE TO HUGH M'DONALD, ESQ. From *Poems and Songs*, Saint John, N.B., 1860.

92 OLD NICK IN SOREL. From *The Emigrant*, Montreal, 1842. One of a number of bits of light verse O'Grady scattered through his copious notes to the poem.

93 RURAL HENHOUSE. From *Poems for All the Annettes*, Toronto, 1962.

95 SONG TO THE FOUR SEASONS. From *Sarah Binks*, Toronto, 1947. The author, a Professor of Chemistry at the University of Manitoba, invented a "sweet singer of Saskatchewan" who must be held responsible for this delightfully atrocious verse.

96 MANITOBA BECOMES A PROVINCE. From *College Days*, Toronto, 1923.

96 THE FARMER AND THE FARMER'S WIFE. From *Sarah Binks*.

97 TO MY FATHER, JACOB BINKS. From *Sarah Binks*.

98 PRAIRIE GRAVEYARD. From *Sandstone*, Toronto, 1945. This bitter study of the depression years in the west is a savage epilogue to Miss Marriott's "The Wind Our Enemy".

99 ESTEVAN, SASKATCHEWAN. From *Trio*, Toronto, 1954.

100 BACKGROUND. From *Under the Ice*, Toronto, 1961.

103 WE LIVE IN A RICKETY HOUSE. From *The Emigrant and Other Poems*, 1861.

103 PRECEPT AND EXAMPLE. From *Poems and Essays*, Montreal, 1874.

104 REV. DR. BELLYGOD. From *Muse Whangs*, Toronto, 1887. The author appended the following amusing note to his poem:

Of the satires on gospel-grinders to be met with in fiction, Peacock's Rev. Drs. Grovelgrub and Opinian are among the best. The Rev. Nathaniel Sneakesby in Reynold's "Court of London" is a character happily conceived and amusingly drawn, and probably intended to represent a type of the Methodist parson not extremely rare. Readers of Stevenson's stories will remember the Rev. Simon Rowles in *New Arabian Nights*, who found his theological books very dull after he had bagged the Rajah's diamond. Perhaps some readers may be diverted by the following anecdote of an amorous minister:—

A reverend divine of olden time, residing in Hamilton, and still remembered there as the famous Dr. S——, had occasion to travel to London frequently. On one of these journeys he arrived at an inn where he had formerly put up, but was informed that the bedrooms were all occupied, and that with the exception of a bed in a double-bedded room, there was no accommodation. The reverend gentleman consented to take the bed; and on retiring was admonished by the housekeeper to keep himself very quiet as a lady occupied the other bed. The doctor, nothing daunted, proceeded to the room, and it being late in the night, silence reigned throughout the inn. Suddenly a shout from the worthy divine alarmed the house—landlord, scullions, and all rushed half-naked to the scene. The shouting grew more distinct. "The lady's dead! The lady's dead!" was distinctly uttered by the divine, which was met by the jeering response of the landlord:—"Who the devil would have thought of putting you in the same room with a living one!"

105 AN ARISTOCRATIC TRIO. From *Muse Whangs*, Toronto, 1887.

106 TWO THOUSAND YEARS OF PREACHING. From the *Canadian Forum*, March, 1947.

106 BREBEUF AND HIS BRETHREN. From *The Eye of the Needle*, Montreal, 1957.

107 TO AN ULTRA PROTESTANT. From *The Poems of Archibald Lampman*, edited with a Memoir by Duncan Campbell Scott, Toronto, 1900.

107 IF I WERE THE DEVIL. From *Place of Meeting*, Toronto, 1960.

108 THE SCEPTIC. From *Rhymes of a Rolling Stone*, 1912.

108 DEACON ARNOLD. From *Comber Cove*, Toronto, 1937.

109 THE IMMIGRANT. From *Place of Meeting*, Toronto, 1960.

109 JESUS SAVES. From *The Black Huntsman*, Toronto, 1951.

110 INSURANCE. From *Place of Meeting*, Toronto, 1960.

110 RESURRECTION OF ARP. First published in *New Verse*, London, 1936; in *News of the Phoenix*, Toronto and New York, 1943. Arp is not the painter.

111 CAROL FOR THE INTERIM. First published in *The Blasted Pine*, 1957.

115 THE CANADIAN AUTHORS MEET. First published in the *McGill Fortnightly Review*, April, 1927; in *Overture*, 1945. Written on the occasion when the author attended a meeting of the local poetry group to see his present collaborator awarded a prize for a piece of sentimental verse.

116 TO THE CANADIAN POETS. From *Unit of 5*, Toronto, 1944.

116 CAN. LIT. From *Ice Cod Bell or Stone*, Toronto, 1962.

117 AND SPOIL THE CHILD. From the *Canadian Forum, 1931*; also in *The Ill-Tempered Lover*, Toronto, 1948.

120 ON READING AN ANTHOLOGY OF POPULAR POETRY. First published in *Poetry* (Chicago); in *News of the Phoenix*, 1943.

121 EPIGRAMME. First published in *The Blasted Pine*, 1957.

121 THE McGILL DAILY. From the *McGill Fortnightly Review*, March 22, 1926.

121 THE TASTE OF SPACE. From *Saturday Night*, November, 1966.

121 THE LAYMAN TURNED CRITIC. First published in *The Blasted Pine*, 1957.

122 CONCOURSE AT CATARAQUI. An impression of the Literary Conference held at Queen's University in the summer of 1955. From *The Improved Binoculars*, Toronto, 1956.

122 THE DEATH OF THE POETESS. From *The Red Heart*, 1949.

123 MISUNDERSTANDING. From *The Long Peashooter*, Toronto, 1954.

124 ON READING CERTAIN POEMS & EPISTLES. These verses grew out of a controversy between the author and Mr. Layton and others in the *Canadian Forum*, 1956-7.

125 TO IRVING LAYTON ON HIS LOVE POEM etc. From *The Canadian Forum.*

125 LINES TO CERTAIN YOUNG CANADIAN POETS. From *A Point of Sky*, Toronto, 1964.

125 A CURSE ON THOSE WHO KISS AND TELL. From *A Radiant Sphere*, Moscow, 1964.

129 WAR ON THE PERIPHERY. From the *New Yorker*, April 21, 1951.

130 THE ANNEXATION OF NATAL. From *College Days*, 1923.

130 ANGLO-JAPANESE ALLIANCE. From *College Days*, 1923.

131 LEST WE FORGET. Written in the early 1930's; in *Overture*, 1945.

132 BATTLE HYMN OF THE SPANISH REBELLION. From the *Canadian Forum*, October, 1936; in *Viper's Bugloss*, by John Smalacombe, Toronto, 1938.

132 TWO SNARLS OF A DISGUSTED COLONIAL. From the *Canadian Forum*, August, 1937.

132 POLITICAL INTELLIGENCE. First published in *Contemporary Poetry and Prose* (London); in *News of the Phoenix*, 1943.

133 KIRKLAND LAKE. First published in *The Book of Canadian Poetry*, edited by A. J. M. Smith, Chicago and Toronto, 1943.

134 THE USE OF FORCE. From the *Canadian Forum*, February, 1940.

134 IN THIS VERANDAH. From *David and Other Poems*, 1942.

135 #70 ARMY RECEPTION CENTRE, FREDERICTON, N.B. From *Place of Meeting*, Toronto, 1960.

136 HERO'S REWARD. From the *Canadian Forum*, April, 1956.

137 PSALM 23. From *Flight Into Darkness*, New York, 1944.

137 ON THE *STRUMA* MASSACRE. The S.S. *Struma*, with 700 Jewish refugees from fascist Romania, was denied passage through the Bosphorus because the British government had not issued passports for Palestine. Sent out to sea with no pilot and no destination she ran into a mine and sank, February 25, 1942. There was one survivor.

138 From *NEW WINGS FOR ICARUS*, Toronto, 1966. Revised by author.

143 OUTMODED WISDOM. From the *Canadian Forum*, April, 1936; in *Viper's Bugloss*, 1938.

144 EURYNOME. From "The Plowman in Darkness", the *Canadian Forum*, March, 1956. In *The Boatman*, Toronto, 1957.

144 HAIL WEDDED LOVE. From the *Canadian Forum*, March, 1956. In *The Boatman*, Toronto, 1957.

145 SOUR WINE. From *The Book of Canadian Poetry*, first edn., 1943.

145 I WISH MY TONGUE. From *Viper's Bugloss*, 1938.

146 A PORTRAIT, AND A PROPHECY. From *News of the Phoenix*, 1943.

146 FREAK SHOW. From *Cerberus*, Toronto, 1952.

147 THE IMPROVED BINOCULARS. From *The Cold Green Element*, Toronto, 1955. Also the title poem of Layton's selected poems, Highlands, North Carolina, 1956.

148 CHRIST WALKS IN THIS INFERNAL DISTRICT TOO. From *Selected Poems of Malcolm Lowry*, San Francisco, 1962.

148 THE CITY OF THE END OF THINGS. From *The Poems of Archibald Lampman*, 1900. This powerful denunciation of a mechanical world seems a fitting conclusion to this anthology.

ACKNOWLEDGEMENTS

Grateful acknowledgements are due to the following publishers, authors and literary executors for the poems listed below:

Margaret Atwood, for "At the Tourist Center in Boston" and "The Lifeless Wife".

Henry Beissel, for "From *New Wings for Icarus*".

Earle Birney, for "Canada: Case History", "Anglosaxon Street", and "In This Verandah".

Fred Cogswell, for "Ode to Fredericton".

John Robert Colombo, for "Found Object" and "On Ostentation".

Louis Dudek, for the Epigraph and for "The Layman Turned Critic".

Robert Finch, for "Epigramme".

Ralph Gustafson, for "On the *Struma* Massacre" and "Psalm 23, Revised Version".

Harvard University Press for "A Church Seen in Canada", from Theodore Spencer *An Acre in the Seed*, copyright 1949 by the President and Fellows of Harvard College.

Michael Hornyansky, for "Carol for the Interim" and "The Penguin".

Vernal House, for "Local Boy".

George Johnston, for "War on the Periphery".

George Jonas, for "For the Record".

J. D. Ketchum, for "Hymn to the Glory of Free Enterprise".

Irving Layton, for "From Colony to Nation", "Golfers", "Anglo-Canadian", "Jesus Saves", "Misunderstanding", and "The Improved Binoculars".

Mrs. Malcolm Lowry for "Christ Walks in this Infernal District Too" by Malcolm Lowry.

McClelland and Stewart Ltd., for "Dialectics" from *The Colour as Naked* (1953) by Patrick Anderson; "Funeral of an Administrator" from *Deeper Into the Forest* (1948) by Roy Daniells; "Listed" from *The Strength of the Hills* (1948) by Robert Finch; "Letter to a Librarian" from *A Laughter of the Mind* (1958), "The Way the World Ends" and "Concourse at Cataraqui" from *The Improved Binoculars* (1956) by Irving Layton; "Business as Usual" and "The Only Tourist in Havana" from *Flowers for Hitler* (1964) by Leonard Cohen: "Can. Lit." and "Sinalóa" from *Ice Cod Bell or Stone* (1962) by Earle Birney; "Homo Canadensis" from *The Cariboo Horses* (1965) by Alfred Purdy.

Wilson MacDonald, for "Deacon Arnold", "The Service Club", and "The Member of Parliament".

L. A. MacKay for "Frankie Went Down to the Corner", "And Spoil the Child", "Battle Hymn of the Spanish Rebellion", "Two Snarls of a Disgusted Colonial", "Outmoded Wisdom", and "I Wish My Tongue Were a Quiver".

E. W. Mandel, for "Estevan, Saskatchewan".

Anne Marriott, for "Prairie Graveyard".

Peter Miller, for "Festival at Stratford".

Mrs. Nimmo, for the three poems of Stephen Leacock entitled "Manitoba Becomes a Province", "The Annexation of Natal", and "Anglo-Japanese Alliance", from *College Days* (1923).

Alden Nowlan, for "Background".

Oxford University Press, for "Song to the Four Seasons", "The Farmer and the Farmer's Wife", and "To My Father, Jacob Binks" from *Sarah Binks* (1947) by Paul Hiebert; "Eurynome" and "Hail Wedded Love" from *The Boatman* (1957) by Jay Macpherson; "Lines to Certain Young Canadian Poets" from *A Point of Sky* by John Glassco.

P. K. Page, for "Election Day" and "Landlady".

Alfred Purdy, for "Rural Henhouse".

James Reaney, for "The Royal Visit", "The Death of the Poetess", and "Le Tombeau de Pierre Falcon".

The Ryerson Press, for "The Monarch of the Id", from *Trial of a City* (1952) by Earle Birney; "Cold Colloquy" from *The White Centre* (1945) by Patrick Anderson; "Political Meeting", "M. Bertrand", and "Monsieur Gaston" from *The Rocking Chair* (1948) by A. M. Klein; "Ballade of Meddlers" from *The Complete Poems* (1922) of Tom MacInnes; "The Canadian Social Register" and "Bonne Entente" from *Events and Signals* (1945) by F. R. Scott; "The Sceptic" and "Five-per-Cent" from *Collected Poems* (1954) by Robert W. Service; "Resurrection of Arp", "Political Intelligence", and "A Portrait and a Prophecy" from *A Sort of Ecstasy* (1954) by A. J. M. Smith.

Mrs. B. K. Sandwell, for "On the Appointment of Governor-General Vincent Massey, 1952" by B. K. Sandwell.

F. R. Scott, for "National Identity".

A. J. M. Smith, for "The Taste of Space" and "To Irving Layton".

Raymond Souster, for "Fredericton", "To the Canadian Poets", "The Enemies", "Freak Show", "Parliamentary Library, Ottawa", "If I Were the Devil", "The Immigrant", "Insurance", and "#70 Army Reception Centre, Fredericton, N.B."

Mrs. George Walton, for "Hero's Reward" and "To a Restless Politician" by George Walton.

Joe Wallace, for "A Sovereign Nation", "Panic", and "A Curse on Those Who Kiss and Tell".

The executors of the late Anne Wilkinson for "Leda in Stratford, Ont."

INDEX OF AUTHORS